HUMAN EXPERIENCE

An Inconvenient Truth

Michael K. Nsah

TABLE OF CONTENTS

The portrayal of Job's life and experience relates to the life and experience of all people who have lived, who are living, and who will ever live on planet Earth.

DEDICATION

This book is dedicated as a tool in the hands of God our Father, our Lord and Savior Jesus Christ, and the Holy Spirit who continues to be our spiritual GPS so that we will not be lost in our quest for the *TRUTH*.

PREFACE

As I walked, reflecting on my life experiences, as most humans do, and asking, 'O God, *where* are you and *why* are you silent?' thoughts began to flood my mind. I had to pull a sticky note pad out of my pocket and begin writing. We often spend a lifetime asking the pressing questions of who we are and where we are at any given moment. Unfortunately, the answers aren't always easily accessible, especially if we aren't rooted in a solid foundation of faith during our most desperate times of need, disappointment, or struggle.

But God, who diligently works out all things according to His wise counsel and knows the end from the beginning, based on our covenant agreement with Him, helps us endure the journey. The journey we call our life experience is marked by a myriad of questions and very few answers.

"Human Experience: An Inconvenient Truth revealed through *Job's* experience, will hopefully become that book—a source of comfort, a place where readers can turn when their lives veer off course, grief feels unrelenting, obstacles seem insurmountable, and God appears *'dead silent.'*

"Human Experience: An Inconvenient Truth" is not merely about *Job's* suffering or the patience of *Job.* It is a story about the *"Job"* in every one of us. It is about all human experience gleaned from the events of *Job's* experience as revealed to him and about his purpose. Like *Job,* we

are greater than we think we are without even knowing it. It is a missing piece of a bigger puzzle: life's meaning and purpose—our human experience wrapped in a mystery.

As adults, we often learn that, sooner or later, regardless of how diligently we plan our futures or stockpile our assets to live out our best lives, perfectly laid plans can and will always find a way to fall apart at the most inopportune times. Pain and suffering are a part of our daily existence, despite our bank balances, affluent home addresses, or six- or seven-figure jobs.

Simply put, there is no path to living a life without some heartbreak and upheaval during our time on this earth. However, with a better understanding of God's life covenant agreement with us through the story of Job, we can effectively arm ourselves with a guided tour—a way through and a way out of our most arduous moments. We must ask, seek, and knock to get the answers He has already provided.

INTRODUCTION

"When God chooses not to engage only humans in His actions on earth according to our covenant agreement with Him, He also incorporates the angels and Satan to execute His sovereign agenda with swift and laser-beam accuracy. Therefore, in the fullness of time, for the dispensation of the events on the Almighty's prophetic calendar, these two agents are His preferred direct channel of operation. This is precisely the case with *Job* and all of *us*! It is the story about our restoration and double blessing."

My sincere hope is that readers of this book will derive a deep and helpful insight into the nature of God and His ways with each of us. I earnestly pray that as we read through the pages, the Holy Spirit will quicken our spiritual understanding of God's love, power, and purpose. May the revelation of Christ Jesus, our Lord, widen our horizons to see beyond the natural.

- Michael K. Nsah

"And the Lord released Job from **captivity** *when he prayed for his friends. Also, the Lord gave Job twice as much as he had before. Then came there unto him all his brethren and all his sisters, and all those who had been his acquaintance before and ate bread with him in his house. And they bemoaned him and comforted him over* **<u>all the evil that the Lord had brought upon him</u>**. *Every man also gave him a piece of money, and everyone an earring of gold. So, the Lord blessed the latter end of Job more than his beginning..."*

Life, in its most fundamental form, is a complex tapestry woven from the threads of countless experiences, emotions, and events. It is a journey that begins with a single, enigmatic moment—the moment of birth. This is the first mystery that we encounter in our existence, a mystery that sets the stage for the myriad of others that will follow.

The moment of birth is a paradox, a confluence of both simplicity and complexity. It is a simple biological process, yet it is also an intricate dance of cells and genes; a symphony of life that is played out in the womb. It is a process that has been repeated billions of times throughout history, yet each occurrence is unique. Each new life is a fresh canvas upon which the story of existence will be painted. Yet the mystery of life's beginnings extends beyond the physical. It delves into the realms of the metaphysical, the spiritual, and the existential. It raises questions that have puzzled philosophers and scientists for centuries.

Where does consciousness come from? What sparks the flame of awareness in a newborn child? Is there a purpose to our existence, a reason for our being? These questions, like the mystery of life's beginnings, are not easily answered. They require introspection, contemplation, and a willingness to delve into the unknown. They challenge our understanding of the world and our place in it. They force us to confront the inconvenient truth of our existence—that we are, in many ways, a mystery to ourselves.

Yet, it is in the pursuit of these answers, in the unraveling of life's enigmatic beginnings, that we truly begin to understand the beauty and complexity of human experience. It is a journey fraught with uncertainty and doubt, but it is also one that is filled with discovery, enlightenment, and a profound sense of awe because the architect and porter of our lives is a master at what He does.

xiv

FROM THE DESK OF PASTOR ALFRED PATRICK UDOBONG:

"Human Experience: An Inconvenient Truth" is a timeless book.

In a time like this, we need a book like this. A good portion of this book is based on practical life experience. Stories are easy to tell, but when it comes to having the experience, it is from the heart of one who has gone through the situation. The author is not telling a story; he is just sharing his life experience and relating it to present-day events.

What you think you know is nothing compared to what you don't know, but God knows all things before they begin and the future before it ever comes into existence. In this book, we are reminded again that the physical world does not control itself. It is controlled by the Spiritual—by God, who made all things, and everything is absolutely in His hands and under His control.

When you think you know all, you have all wrapped up in your sleeves and ready to go, and you suddenly realize His plans are higher, His ways are perfect despite the pains, His understanding is beyond imagination, and His wisdom is excellent regardless of the length of time it takes to unfold itself. I wish Christians, in particular, would know that God is far ahead of us, and when we submit to Him, He will guide us through even the most difficult times. 'I am the way and the truth and the life. Without me, you can do nothing.'

His ways are far from ours, and the best way to get there is to follow Him submissively. Job wrote: "Indeed, I know that this is true. But how can mere mortals prove their innocence before God? Though they wished to dispute with him, they could not answer him once out of a thousand. His wisdom is profound; his power is vast."

Who has resisted him and come out unscathed? He moves mountains without their knowing it and overturns them in his anger. He shakes the earth from its place and makes its pillars tremble. He speaks to the sun, and it does not shine; he seals off the light of the stars. He alone stretches out the heavens and treads on the sea's waves. He is the Maker of the Bear and Orion, the Pleiades, and the constellations of the South. He performs wonders that cannot be fathomed, miracles that cannot be counted. When he passes me, I cannot see him; when he goes by, I cannot perceive him. If he snatches away, who can stop him? Who can say to him, 'What are you doing?'"

This book is a firsthand account of the author's life; it is not a narrative from a distance or one learned from others. It is a personal experience, a godly one, and doctrinal. It will light a fire in your heart to desire Christ Jesus as your Lord and Savior. You will always need a book like this to rest your hope on, knowing that the future is assured through Christ Jesus and that this future will surely come. This book will strike a chord in you to trust God. It will help you gain a better understanding of what salvation is and how to trust and follow Christ Jesus.

The author of this book is a busy man, a busy child of the living God. However, you would not know when you meet him because of his humility and unhurried, truly engaging manners, being transformed by the spirit of God through Christ our Lord. He is a man who seeks, desires, and fervently prays for the salvation of souls. He prays that you will grow to know God and Christ Jesus, whom He sent into the world for all humanity to see God in the flesh. He carries this responsibility with a sense of divine mandate and urgency.

As you read this book, you see yourself in the light of God guiding you every step, every day, and everywhere. Like *Job*, you will sense He never departs from you for a second; you will realize He needs you more than you need Him; and you will realize He is forever committed to being faithful to His words and promises.

What makes this book profound and relevant is how the writer includes insights into his personal life experience with Bible references, giving the reader hope and assurance of a better future as they navigate everyday life. This book is not centered on oneself but on Christ, what He has done, and what He will do. *"Human Experience: An Inconvenient Truth,"* by Michael K. Nsah, is a pleasure to read. It will multiply grace and give hope for the reader to know that the future has so much more in store than the present.

Pastor Alfred Patrick Udobong
Global Manifestations Ministries
Lynchburg, VA,
USA

RECOMMENDATION

Michael has been a dear friend of mine for several years, and I have had the privilege of witnessing his unwavering passion and dedication to understanding the complexities of human experience. His book, *"Human Experience: An Inconvenient Truth,"* is a testament to his intellectual depth and his profound empathy for others. Michael's insatiable curiosity and tireless pursuit of knowledge shine through every page as he delves into what it means to be human.

What truly sets Michael apart is his ability to bridge the gap between academia and everyday life. He effortlessly combines rigorous research with personal anecdotes, creating a narrative that is both intellectually stimulating and emotionally resonant. Through his eloquent prose, Michael invites readers to embark on a transformative journey, challenging conventional wisdom and prompting us to question the very essence of our existence. His book is a testament to his profound insights and his remarkable ability to distill complex concepts into accessible and relatable ideas.

"Human Experience: An Inconvenient Truth" is not just a book; it reflects Michael's deep compassion and his genuine desire to make a positive impact on the world. His unique perspective challenges us to embrace discomfort and confront inconvenient truths about ourselves and society. I am confident that Michael's book will leave an indelible mark on anyone who reads it, sparking introspection, fostering empathy, and

ultimately inspiring us to strive for a more meaningful and authentic human experience.

Michael's strong belief in God and his role as a minister have undoubtedly played a pivotal role in shaping his perspective and guiding his writing of *"Human Experience: An Inconvenient Truth."* His faith serves as a steady anchor, providing him with the moral compass and spiritual depth necessary to delve into profound questions of human existence. It is through his connection with the divine that Michael finds inspiration, solace, and a profound sense of purpose, which shines through every word of his book. His unwavering faith infuses the pages with a sense of hope and meaning, inviting readers to explore the profound mysteries of life while encouraging a deeper understanding of human experience in the context of a larger, spiritual narrative.

Michael's unique ability to blend his intellectual prowess with his deep spirituality makes this book a compelling and transformative read for individuals seeking not only intellectual enlightenment but also a deeper connection with their spirituality.

I highly recommend this book as a valuable addition to your library.

Dr. David J. Knight Sr.,
Atlanta, Georgia

FOREWORD

"It is an honor to recommend 'Human Experience: An Inconvenient Truth,' written and lived by my dear friend and faithful Christ-follower, Michael K. Nsah. Michael lays out a powerful template for navigating the suffering and pain in life that he has faced, one that leads to the greatest of healings, and fighting spiritually through life's battles to achieve the sweetest of victories. Michael dares to challenge us to also believe and trust God's greater purpose for our lives, despite the inevitable setbacks we all face in our life journey. *"Human Experience: An Inconvenient Truth"* is a book long overdue to help hurting humanity face and overcome our struggling culture and chaotic life."

Dr. Jim L. Bolin
Bishop, Seven Springs Churches,
Greater Atlanta, GA

ACKNOWLEDGMENTS

For all the remarkable people who have impacted my life through the years. Without them, I wouldn't have had testimony.

This book is also dedicated to my parents, Elder Kanu Nwa Kanu Nsah and Sarah Obonugwa Kanu Nsah. It is through them that my journey into this world began to fulfill my covenant agreement with God. To my maternal grandfather, Aba Abiom Oberu Aribiah, a.k.a. "Aba Clerk" or "Papa," whose unwavering discipline, rooted in love and faith, guided by the desire to do good for humanity, has shaped my life's principles. As a District Officer (D.O.), Papa traveled extensively throughout the eastern region of Nigeria, earning a reputation as a highly respected civil servant.

Their best, caring, loving, and humble beginnings, but a proud one, established my foundation. Additionally, my aunts and uncle, Mayen Aribiah-Obong, Ndarake Archibong, also known as Nke, and Oberu Aribiah, also known as Kaka, rightfully deserve to share in the dedication of this book. Mayen, Nke, and Kaka were the most significant people, the cornerstones, who took over the baton from my parents and provided me with everything that I needed as a youth and much more. With them in my life, the effect of the loss of my parents at a young age—seven and nine—was very minimal, to say the least. I was truly blessed to have them at each of their appointed seasons in my life.

I must also thank my aunt, Dr. Mary Aribiah, who painstakingly reviewed every page of the manuscript to ensure that the book accurately captured what I intended to share. Her candid feedback as an author herself was invaluable. She always encouraged me to go ahead and publish the book to help others who are seeking explanations for their life experiences.

My heartfelt gratitude must go to Michael Nwaneri, MD, my constant *barometer,* for his steady challenge and push to delay it no more, so that someone else can be blessed with the answers to the questions about their life's *"Whys."*

My deepest appreciation goes to Mrs. M. N. Onyekaba (Mama, also known as Akaenyi) for her unwavering faith. Her generosity, kindness, and grace are a testament to God's love and mercy. Her constant encouragement to stay humble, remain committed, strive for excellence, and make a positive impact has been truly impactful.

Finally, I extend my heartfelt appreciation to my best friend, Bruce Williams, who is always on his knees interceding for "Human Experience: An Inconvenient Truth" to become a reality and to bless others. Without such effectual, fervent prayers and encouragement, this book wouldn't be in your hands today.

CHAPTER 1

An Appointed Time of Obscurity

"There is an appointed time for everything, and there is a time for every event under heaven." - Ecclesiastes 3

There always comes an "appointed time" when God shields you for Himself. During this period, He accomplishes what He desires in you, for you, and through you according to His purpose and your agreement with Him.

A Time and Place of Obscurity

The period when God shields you is a time of obscurity. It is a time when nobody recognizes you for anything that you do. A period when you are unknown; you are undervalued; you are unappreciated, no matter what you do; you are forgotten by virtually everyone you consider friends, even family. A time when no one calls or texts because you have nothing of significance to offer. A lonely wilderness where your only connection, if you are aware of Him, is God. A place of intense discomfort, known in part as our *"Human Experience."*

No one prays or desires to be in a place of obscurity. Yet it inevitably comes uninvited and unwelcome. You have probably been to that place. Or you're there now. If not, you will be someday. It's a place and time when nothing 'positive' seems to happen to you. However, know that the seed of a mighty oak tree first gets buried in the dark soil for a while to develop its roots before springing out to be seen as an oak tree. The most beautiful photographs used to be created only in the darkroom. It is a period when God ensures that you are entirely reliant on Him, with reckless abandon. Men and women like Abraham, Jacob, Moses, Joseph, David, Ruth, Elijah, Esther, Mary Slessor, Oswald Chambers, Abraham Lincoln, Lewis Latimer, Henry Dunant, Mother Teresa, Dr. Martin Luther King, Nelson Mandela, T.D. Jakes, Steve Jobs, Oprah Winfrey, and Tyler Perry, to name a few, were obscure until the fullness of time came for them to be revealed.

This period is often referred to as *"The Day of the Lord"* or our *'Darkest Days'*—the time of our *Job experience*. It is when God reveals another dimension of Himself. It is similar to how the negative terminal of a battery complements the positive terminal. Each terminal alone is insufficient, but together, they ignite the vehicle's engine, fulfilling its purpose. Our *Job experience* serves a similar function in our lives. Lessons learned in obscurity prepare you for a greater purpose.

When God permitted Satan to test *Job*, his wife could not understand God's ultimate purpose for her husband or their family. She questioned the rationale behind *Job's* faith, even urging him to *"Curse God and die."* *Job's* response was quite telling: *"Shall we receive good from God and not receive evil?"* or *"Shall we receive only pleasant things from God and never anything unpleasant?"*

Job's experience, as narrated in the first two chapters of the Book of Job, offers us a glimpse into heaven's council room—the invisible realm where the Trinity and the hosts of heaven dwell. From this council room, the Almighty dispatches angels to implement His agenda for all dispensations.

Heaven's Supreme Council: First Meeting

In the supreme conference room in heaven, a highly anticipated special assignments deployment meeting is about to begin. Angels, dressed in white robes, arrive on time and take their assigned seats.

The angelic servants in heaven are on standby in case they are needed to serve the meeting attendees. You can hear a pin drop as the sound of His Majesty's steps echoes in the corridors. The Supreme Commander of Heaven and Earth, the Supreme Chief Justice of the Universe, is making His way from the back gallery into the gothic conference room.

Suddenly, the majestic double-leaf doors swing open, and the Royal Majesty, in the effulgence of His glory, walks in. All present rise and bow in His honor. He takes His seat. All is set. His commanding presence fills the conference chamber; all attendees have their eyes fixed on Him.

After welcoming the audience, God begins to flip through the open book placed before Him, presumably reading the log of predetermined assignments for every living person. The angels, ready to update their records, begin reporting back to God on their last assignments. After the reports, God calls on each angel and reads out specific assignments for the day.

Moments later, Satan, dressed in a full black robe, enters the room, late as usual, and takes his seat at the left side of the conference table. The angels are focused with rapt attention on the throne, where His Majesty is sitting, to avoid missing any detail of their assignments. They do not notice Satan's arrival. But the Omniscient is aware. Satan's presence is not unusual; he is a regular participant in these heavenly joint sessions, strictly by God's invitation.

Once the angels receive their instructions, they joyously compare assignments and exit the room. Satan, anxious for his turn, begins pacing up and down. Unbeknownst to him, *Job* is at the top of God's list of assignments.

Based on *Job's* covenant agreement with God long before he was formed in his mother's womb, this was his appointed time and day. Consider also that when the fullness of time came for the birth of our Savior, all infant boys two years old and under were killed by King Herod's decree, prompting baby Jesus to flee to Egypt. When John the Baptist's time came to an end, he was beheaded due to a promise made by Herod to Herodias' daughter. These events and their implications were not coincidental but part of our heavenly Father's agreement. They were intricately woven into their painful human experiences.

When Jesus' time to be crucified approached, Peter tried to prevent Him, but Jesus rebuked him, saying, *"Get thee behind me, Satan."* Nothing could have stopped Judas from betraying Jesus on that fateful evening, as it was the predetermined time. Similarly, *Job's* trials were appointed by God. Just as Satan was present at the meeting in heaven to be deployed to *Uz* to test *Job*, he was around the corner on the night of the Last Supper, waiting to enter Judas for his assignment.

Though Jesus had the power to summon twelve legions of angels, He humbled Himself, forsaken by His Father, and laid down His life. With laser beam precision, all the events in our lives are at the appointed time to which we agreed with our heavenly Father. Not even a minor headache comes outside of its appointed time.

Our Father is a master of minute details. From the precise moment that the Serpent approached Eve in the Garden of Eden to the time he entered Judas Iscariot during the Last Supper, and everything in between up to this day, is according to the dispensation of the fullness of their times. It is the fine print in our covenant agreement.

Job's Appointed Time

It is essential to note that angels are constantly coming and going, both in heaven and on earth, fulfilling their duties as directed by God. It is a daily occurrence (from 12:00 a.m. to 11:59 p.m.) for the angels. They are actively ascending and descending between heaven and earth. The significance of this deployment meeting lies in the fact that *Job* is the subject between God and Satan.

This time, the hosts of heaven are attending to bear witness. Satan is specifically given a unique mandate to execute this assignment. It is extraordinary because of the unprecedented magnitude of the outcome.

Typically, *Job* is busy with his routine—worshiping God and praying for his family. Nothing unusual was anticipated. However, on a beautiful day that turns disastrous, a series of well-coordinated tragedies strikes *Job's* family and possessions.

First, the Sabeans attacked, killing his herdsmen and stealing his oxen and donkeys. Then, a fire consumes his sheep and herdsmen. Next, the Chaldeans raid and take his camels, killing more herdsmen. Finally, a *whirlwind* destroys his oldest son's house, killing all of *Job's* children and their attendants.

Amidst this chaos, *Job* remained steadfast. Despite his wife's plea to curse God, he declared, 'I came naked from my mother's womb, and I shall have nothing when I leave this earth and *return to God*. The Lord gave me everything that I have, and He can take it all away. Blessed be the name of the Lord.' Even in his adversity, *Job* refrained from sinning against God or speaking ill of Him. His unwavering faith is a testament to his belief in God's control over his affairs.

In each of our life experiences, we are but threads, intricately woven into the complex patterns of existence. Our lives are a series of puzzles, each one more enigmatic than the last. The mystery of human experience is a labyrinth of questions, a maze of uncertainties, and a riddle of paradoxes. It is a journey of discovery, a quest for understanding, and a pursuit of truth.

The inconvenient truth about the mystery of human experience is that each person's experience is unique and shaped by their perceptions, beliefs, and circumstances. This complexity makes it challenging for humans to comprehend or quantify fully—a truth often overlooked or ignored, yet a crucial aspect of our existence.

Moreover, the human experience is not always pleasant or easy. It is filled with hardships, pain, and questions. But it is also filled with joy, love, and beauty. It is a paradox that is difficult to comprehend, but it is a part of our reality.

The first puzzle of existence is the question of identity. Who are we? Are we merely physical beings, or do we possess a spiritual essence that transcends our corporeal form? Are we the sum of our experiences, or does our potential define us? The answer lies in the delicate balance between our tangible reality and our intangible aspirations. We are both the sculptor and the sculpture, constantly shaping and being shaped by our experiences.

The second puzzle is the enigma of purpose. Why are we here? Is there a grand design to our existence, or are we simply the product of cosmic randomness?

The third puzzle is the conundrum of connection. How do we relate to others and the world around us? Are we isolated entities, or are we interconnected parts of a larger whole? From God's bird's-eye view, the answer lies in our capacity for empathy and compassion.

We are not solitary islands but parts of a vast ocean, with each wave affecting the other and each ripple influencing the whole. Decoding the puzzles of existence is not about finding definitive answers but about embracing the questions. It is about acknowledging the mystery of our existence and celebrating the wonder of our human experience.

It is about living with curiosity, courage, and compassion, and recognizing that the inconvenient truth of life is not its uncertainty but its infinite possibilities. *Job* forgot, just as we have forgotten.

It is about exploring the depths of our consciousness and the boundaries of our existence. It is about questioning, seeking, and finding. It is about embracing the unknown and uncertainty. It is a journey that is filled with revelations. Sometimes, it is both fascinating and terrifying.

Life's journey is filled with challenges. Challenges that test our strength, resilience, and faith. The trials we face, like *Job's*, are meant to refine us and draw us closer to God. They remind us that while we may not control the events in our lives, we can trust in God's plan and purpose for us to be worked out day by day.

Our *Job* experiences, though painful, are part of the divine design to bring glory to God and fulfillment to our lives. As we navigate these trials, let us remember that God is with us, guiding us every step of the way.

CHAPTER 2

The Assignment and the Test

"Great ability backed by experience develops and reveals itself increasingly with every new assignment." - Baltasar Gracian, a Spanish philosopher.

Suddenly, God asks Satan, 'Where have you come from and what have you been up to lately?'

In response, Satan answers, 'I have been patrolling the earth, going back and forth—east to west—and walking up and down—north to south—supervising the hosts of the demons' work, plus wrapping up on my last assignments.'

Upon hearing Satan's response, God poses another question: 'Have you considered my servant *Job*? As you know, he is the most faithful of all men on the planet. He loves and fears me and has nothing to do with evil.' The Almighty is declaring that *Job* is His beloved son, with whom He is well pleased, just as He declared about His pattern Son, our Lord and Savior.

Satan halts abruptly, his face reflecting bewilderment. With his eyes fixed on the floor, he slowly turns toward God, a delighted expression crossing his face. Pausing, Satan muses, "It could be the most crucial deployment of my life and ministry." Then he responds to God, 'Really? Isn't Job's devotion and integrity towards you a result of your protection from me all these years, ensuring that everything he owns remains out of my reach? You have prospered him, rewarded him generously, and bestowed immense wealth upon him. If you do not believe me, remove your protection from his family and possessions and see if he will not curse you to your face.'

'Alright,' says God. 'Have at it as you please. Everything he owns is at your disposal, including his children. Only make sure that you do not touch or hurt him personally.'

Satan beams as he exclaims, 'Oh yes! I've finally secured one of the best deals of my life and ministry!' He bolts out of the meeting chamber in a flash to commence this once-in-a-lifetime assignment.

As Satan hurries out of the presence of the Almighty, he immediately begins to strategize with his special legion of demons. He and his cohorts are on the countdown to strike at *Job's* family and possessions—the prime targets. The task at hand is of high importance, so Satan decides to hand-pick his highest-ranking and most talented elite team of demons.

The execution of this assignment must be flawless, and the demons are fully aware that anything short of perfect execution spells doom for them. The game plan is to execute the attack in successive orders, with no room for errors and no time for *Job* to recover.

The appointed time arrived. *Job* had no clue about what had taken place in Heaven between God, the angels, and Satan, particularly the conversation between God and Satan concerning him.

Job was on his routine schedule, minding his daily business—worshiping God and praying for his children and family. Nothing else was required of him by God to change the outcome of his or his family's daily lives.

No amount of planning, preparation, revelation, wisdom, vision, prayer, or fasting would have prevented what was coming *Job's* way. Summarizing *Job's* life: He did honorable deeds, prayed to God for himself and his family, offered sacrifices to atone for his sins and his children's sins, and then received favors from God. He continued to prosper. Life was good! Therefore, nothing unusual was anticipated.

The entire day was beautiful. The sun was bright, and the sky was perfectly blue. Later, as the sun began to set, *Job's* oldest son's birthday party and celebration were just getting started at his house. In attendance were his six brothers and three sisters, as usual. Then suddenly, a series of well-coordinated tragedies struck, turning the perfect day into the beginning of a horrendous nightmare no human had ever experienced in one day.

The five hundred oxen and five hundred donkeys that were seen resting peacefully moments ago are now running wild in all directions.

The Sabeans had invaded and raided the farmland, killing all the herdsmen except one servant who outran the raiders to break the news to *Job*.

Right then, another tragedy struck. A huge billow of fire was burning everything in its path on the northwest side of *Job's* estate. Only one servant escaped to tell *Job*: 'The fire of God has fallen from Heaven, burning and consuming everything in its path. The sheep and the herdsmen are all dead. I am the only one alive to bring you the news.'

Job, afraid as the fast-moving fireball seemed to be heading toward his estate, saw the fire suddenly contained without human intervention. As *Job* grappled with the news of the fire, his three thousand camels and herdsmen were being slaughtered by the Chaldeans. The only surviving herdsman dashed in to break the news to *Job* in person.

'Oh my God, not again,' cried *Job* in a loud voice that could be heard some distance away. The bewilderment on his face spoke more than words could utter. The beautiful day quickly turned into a doomsday with one calamity after another. Without warning or signs of inclement weather, a mighty whirlwind from the desert swept across the land of *Uz* and ripped through *Job's* oldest son's house, killing his seven sons, three daughters, and all the servants attending the party.

The only surviving servant delivered the final unwelcome news to *Job*, "Your oldest son's house has just collapsed due to the whirlwind, killing your seven sons, three daughters, and all the servants in attendance. I am the only surviving witness to tell you about the incident."

How could *Job's* ten children and most of his servants die such violent deaths? *Job* thought such deaths were reserved for the wicked, not the righteous. *Job's* estate, known as the epicenter of joy and happiness, suddenly turned into a mourners' estate. Visibly shaken, *Job* called for help from neighbors to no avail. It was every man for himself. Finally, he calmed down, stepped out into the yard, lifted his hands, and looked up into the sky, tears streaming down his face as he sobbed. Then he yelled out, 'O God, *why?* Where are you? Please help me.'

Job wished he were dreaming, so he would wake up and be relieved from the nightmare. But it was his reality. Nevertheless, God was overseeing every moment, watching over *Job* with fatherly love behind the scenes. Never doubt that God is very involved in your daily struggles. The ultimate end is to bring Him glory as He reveals Himself to you and draws many closer to Him.

Exhausted, *Job* withdrew into his bedroom and continued to grieve. Moments later, he tore his robes, fell to the floor, and buried his face between his knees. He began to worship God, saying, "I came naked from my mother's womb; I shall have nothing when I leave this earth and return to God. The Lord gave me everything I have, and He can take it all away. Blessed be the name of the Lord."

Even amidst adversity, *Job* remained steadfast, refraining from sinning against the Lord or speaking ill of his God. However, being human, what thoughts might cross his mind regarding God after enduring such distressing news in a single day? His dependence on God is evident. He didn't call his wife, relatives, or friends first. He cried to God and gave thanks.

What we go through can be tough, stretching us beyond our human pain threshold. In our trials and tribulations, we must believe that God is in complete control of the affairs of all creatures, visible and invisible. Indeed, *Job* manages to catch a break, but it is not to last.

This type of conversation occurs daily (between God, the angels, and Satan) in Heaven (the spiritual realm) concerning every man and woman living on earth. Hence, this experience applies to every person who has lived, is living now, or will ever live on Earth—at any point in their earthly journey.

It is essential to note that God initiated faith in Christ through Abraham as the root. But *Job* was before Abraham. Therefore, *Job*, who doesn't have his beginnings with Abraham, has his origins with Adam. Abraham is also included in the lineage of Adam, as is *Job*. All humans are included in Adam. Abraham went through his *Job* experience as evidenced in his life journey.

Heaven's business operates around the clock every day of the year. It is happening even as you are reading this. Angels are ascending and descending between heaven and earth. We learned some critical lessons from Daniel's experience when he prayed and fasted for answers from heaven. The encounter between Angel Gabriel is quite instructive.

Where was Angel Gabriel coming from when the Prince of Persia confronted him? Angel Gabriel had just attended the assignment deployment meeting for the day with the hosts of heaven. He was on his way to deliver the answers to Daniel's prayers as one of his assignments for that day. At the same time, en route to Daniel, the Prince of Persia withstood him for twenty-one days.

Just as *Job* had no idea about what was going on in heaven, Daniel did not know about the battle that was raging in mid-heaven on his behalf between the Prince of Persia and the Angel Gabriel. Thankfully, in Daniel's case, heaven's reinforcement by Angel Michael provided the desperately needed backup for the rescue operation. We, like Daniel, don't know many times why our prayers are not answered immediately and what heaven must do to ensure the delivery of the answers to our prayers each day.

There was another critically important meeting day for assignments. The day that God dispatched Angel Gabriel and tasked him with going to Mary to deliver the news, and the entire process concerning the birth of Jesus. It was in the fullness of time as determined and agreed upon with His Son. With God, details matter.

Therefore, the time, place, who is involved, their role, and even the method of operation matter a great deal in fulfilling our covenant agreement. We may not see the whole picture, especially during the period of our *'Job'* experience, when our memory, patience, thought process, or sense of reason fail us as we are in survival mode. *Job's* reactions confirm what a normal person (flesh and blood) would do.

This scene is a vivid depiction of how the spiritual realm determines and controls the physical realm.

CHAPTER 3

Timing and Location

With God, timing and location are everything.

Times and seasons are critical factors in our human experience.

The human experience, in all its complexity and diversity, is not a random assortment of events but a meticulously orchestrated symphony. The conductor of this symphony is our Father—the God of Timing—who ensures that nothing happens by accident. Every joy, sorrow, triumph, and defeat we encounter is part of a grander design.

These events are not random occurrences but carefully planned, each with a specific purpose designed to shape and mold us into the individuals we are meant to become. They are the tools with which the divine craftsman shapes the raw material of our souls into works of His divine art. The timing of these events is not arbitrary. There is a divine schedule that governs the unfolding of our lives. Every event, no matter how insignificant it may seem, happens at the precise moment it is meant to. There are no delays, no accidents, and no coincidences. Everything unfolds precisely when and as it should.

This inconvenient truth often proves challenging for us to embrace. We like to believe that we are the masters of our destinies and that we control our lives. But the reality is that we are partially in control. We are co-authors of our own stories. We are characters in a divine narrative written by the God of Timing. It does not mean that we are mere puppets manipulated by a divine puppeteer. On the contrary, we are active participants in the unfolding of our stories.

We have the freedom to make choices and shape our destinies in partnership with God. So, the timing of our choices and the events that shape our lives are not completely in our hands alone. It also involves God, who ensures that nothing happens by accident. It is according to our agreement with Him before we left heaven and came to the earthly realm.

The Meaning of 'Job' and the Land of 'Uz'

To aid our understanding of some of *Job's* '*whys*,' we must delve into the meaning of *Job* and why the geographic location of *Uz*, where *Job* and his family lived, was chosen as the setting for his experience.

According to Abarim Publications, the Hebrew word for *Job* is IYOWB, which has many connotations, including 'the hated, the persecuted for being of an opposite tribe; enemy, calamity, the afflicted, or adversity; endurance, a coming back, a returning, he who returns, one restored to one's senses, and restored to perfection.' There are many derivatives of *Job's* name, and he was the greatest of all the men of the East. The East depicts where the sun rises to rule the day and control the day's advancements.

Interestingly, *Job's* name is mentioned fifty-six times in the entire Book of Job. If we let the meaning interpret his name, it means that Job is a man perfected by resurrection or perfected through afflictions to a new beginning. It is important to note that God pays particular attention to numbers. Numbers convey profound messages in His economy and prophetic operations relative to human experience. As our age increases, our human experience changes accordingly. We are expected to think, behave, and see things differently. Job's experience was no different. At the appointed time and age, God ensured that he was in the place appropriate for his experience to be accomplished according to his covenant agreement.

The Almighty, in His infinite sovereignty, chose the land of Uz as the theater for His agenda in Job's life. Why *Uz*? The meaning of *Uz* tells us why. *Uz* means fertile, fruitful, counsel, contemplation, divine plan, inner strength, and power. We notice that the meaning of Uz covers different spectrums or attributes relative to God's purpose. God could have chosen a different geographic location to execute Job's experience, but He would not violate His agreement with Job. And *Uz* was the perfect location. We learn a lot about God's purpose and intention by paying attention to His choices, timing, and locations.

When God formed Adam from the dust of the ground, He determined that the "dust" in which the Omniscient God enclosed Adam would become fertile, fruitful, productive, thriving, flourishing, blooming, bountiful, generative, lush, creative, inventive, and yielding—where His divine plan would be made manifest. Hence, this temple or body in which we dwell, formed from the dust of the ground, is where He is fulfilling His divine purpose—our *Job experience*. God could have simply decreed for man to appear as He did with light and other elements. Instead, He used the dust of the earth to form man. Moreover, every mineral found in the earth's ground is also contained in our bodies. Hence, when cultivated and nurtured, our bodies become fertile, fruitful, and blessed to glorify the Creator.

Examples of God's Choice of Timing and Location

To illustrate God's choice of timing and location:

• *Abraham:* Left Luz to begin his journey to a land whose maker and builder is God.

• *Isaac:* Egypt, where the promise was fulfilled according to God's prophetic timetable.

• *Jacob:* Wrestled with God at Peniel, where he broke his thigh and had his name changed to Israel.

• *Joseph:* From the pit to Egypt—Potiphar's house as a slave, prison, and eventually the palace as second in command.

• *Moses:* Egypt—Nile River, palace, burning bush, and deliverer.

- *Ruth:* A Moabite in Bethlehem, meeting Boaz (the lineage of our Lord Jesus Christ).

- *David:* From shepherd boy to defeating Goliath, hiding in caves, and eventually becoming Israel's most beloved king, a man after God's heart.

- *Esther:* A Jewish orphan who became queen in Shushan.

- *Einstein:* Survived the Holocaust, found refuge in the United States, and became a renowned scientist.

- *Nelson Mandela:* Survived 27 years in prison to become president of South Africa.

From Abraham to Jesus Christ, passing through David, God's timing and chosen locations intersect with people and events, all contributing to the coherence of our covenant with Him. To comprehend the full scope, we must connect the dots, bridging our past to our present to grasp the complete picture.

If you have been written off by society, family, friends, acquaintances, etc., and labeled as one who would amount to nothing, then cheers and welcome to *Job's company.* Your greatness is about to be revealed through the knowledge you will gain after reading the mystery of *"Human Experience: An Inconvenient Truth." Job* thought he was the greatest man among all the men from the East. His influence extended beyond his native *Uz.* His three friends traveled from different countries to visit and console him. But after his encounter with the

Omnipotent One, he realized his greatness far exceeded his, his friends, and his family's opinions of him.

The *"Human Experience"* is a story about *Job* and all of *us*. With God, the pathway to your greatness is through the valley of the shadow of death. In that valley, He allows you to learn to fear no evil. He promises to be with you and ensure you make it victoriously to your double portion inheritance because He has guaranteed it with His blood and His life.

Human experience is a complex tapestry of emotions, thoughts, and actions woven together by the threads of time and circumstance. It is a journey as unique as it is universal, a mystery as profound as it is mundane. Yet, despite its complexity and unpredictability, it is possible to master the art of human experience.

Mastering the art of human experience is not about achieving perfection or avoiding pain. It is about learning to navigate the ebb and flow of life with grace, resilience, and wisdom. It is about cultivating a deep sense of self-awareness that is rooted in God through Christ, understanding our emotions, and learning to respond rather than react to the challenges life throws our way.

This mastery begins with acceptance—accepting our strengths and weaknesses, our triumphs and failures, our joys and sorrows. It is about acknowledging the full spectrum of our human experience without judgment or resistance. This acceptance allows us to embrace our humanity in all its messy glory and paves the way for growth and transformation.

Next, we must cultivate mindfulness. Mindfulness is the practice of being fully present at each moment, observing our thoughts, feelings, and sensations without getting caught up in them. It is about stepping back from the drama of life and witnessing it with curiosity and compassion. This mindful awareness can help us navigate life's ups and downs with greater ease and equanimity. Finally, mastering the art of human experience involves cultivating compassion for us and others.

It means the ability to feel with others, to understand their pain and joy, and to respond with kindness and care. It is about recognizing our shared humanity and extending our love and support to those around us. In essence, mastering the art of human experience is about living fully and deeply, embracing the mystery of life with open hearts and minds. It is about learning to dance with life even when the music is out of tune. It is about finding beauty in the chaos, wisdom in the confusion, and love in the midst of it all.

CHAPTER 4

Purpose

"There is no greater agony in life than bearing an untold story inside you." -
Maya Angelou, Author

The power of our purpose engineers all things.

Heaven's Supreme Council: Second Meeting

In the invisible realm of Heaven, a second special deployment meeting is about to begin. Each meeting follows a familiar pattern, including Satan's habitual tardiness and restless pacing. Only the Omniscient knows what lies ahead. Once again, *Job* is the focal point of discussion between God and Satan. (Who among us might be the focus of today's meeting in heaven?)

This experience will bring Job to the brink of unfathomable pain, woes, and misery, unprecedented in human history. Following the previous meeting's outcome—*Job's* loss of all possessions and children—the stakes are higher. The sovereignty of the Supreme Commander of Heaven's Armies is absolute, and no one dares question Him. Every assignment must be executed precisely as instructed without deviation. These assignments reflect the recipients' covenant for the day, unveiling the mystery of the inconvenient truth we deal with.

Satan is more anxious than before. His flawless execution in the previous assignment left *Job* and his family in complete devastation, wiping out all his possessions and killing his ten children, sparing only his wife. Despite his anxiety, Satan is secretly delighted by his previous success.

The Conversation Between God and Satan

Job probably believes he can now heave a sigh of relief as he mourns his tragic losses. Sadly, his trials are far from over. Just like in the previous meeting, *Job* is at the top of God's list for Satan. God initiates the conversation again, asking Satan the same questions and reiterating Job's faithfulness. Satan's activities on earth remain unchanged as he continues seeking whom he may devour.

God asks, "Have you considered my servant *Job*? He is the most faithful of all men on the planet. He loves and fears Me and has nothing to do with evil. He kept his faith and trust in Me, even though you instigated *Me to let you* destroy his family and possessions without any justification." Satan replies, 'Oh well, Your Majesty, skin for skin—a man will give anything to save his life. Just *let me* touch his body with sickness, and he will certainly curse you to your face. I guarantee it.'

The Lord says to Satan, 'Do as you please to his flesh and body, but do not touch his life (do not kill him). *His breath is mine.*' The Omniscient must have His reasons for repeating the same line of conversation with Satan on both occasions.

Job Cries Out Bitterly to God

Preston Eby's "The Secret of *Job*" describes *Job's* experience: "Now it is God who deliberately hands *Job* over, the perfect and righteous man, unto Satan to do his worst upon him. The no-go area is not to touch his life. God permits Satan to administer his worst afflictions, blow by blow, upon *Job* to the extent that he is purified as gold in the end. It was not Satan's idea to persecute poor old *Job*! Oh no! God Himself initiated it!"

The ordeal of *Job's* experience is genuinely a mystery unfolding in real-time. It is wisdom portrayed as a fable, a riddle, or a proverb, often presented in poetic drama. It penetrates the human soul where facts, reason, and logic cannot explain. It is evident from *Job's* experience that Satan is one of God's most obedient servants who thoroughly understands authority. He immediately dashes out of the Almighty's presence to execute this diabolical assignment on *Job's* health with precision.

This assignment is so significant that Satan decides to handle it himself and not delegate any part of it to the rank-and-file demons. He determines that this assignment must yield maximum impact.

Satan takes pleasure and derives fulfillment from human misery. However, in the end, Job's experience is played out in the natural realm to fulfill his agreement that was sealed in heaven.

Based on *Job's* reactions and maintaining his faith in God, Satan figures he needs to inflict more severe damage to drive Job to deny or curse God. Even *Job's* wife becomes Satan's human mouthpiece and agent against her husband. The purpose of the experience is to push *Job* to the extent that his faith is tested and to reveal his heart. It also validates God's omniscient wisdom and demonstrates that Satan takes pleasure in human misery.

However, beyond the natural, *Job* was a man ruled by the spirit of fear; likely unknown to him but known to God. That is why *Job* was always praying for his children and offering sacrifices, fearing they might have sinned against God. *Job* lived in constant fear of failure, suffering, and death. On the surface, everything seemed perfectly okay in *Job's* life, but he did not have peace. *Job* was not a free man. He worried about his possessions, children, and life.

When he was stripped of everything, *Job* finally confessed, *"For the thing which I greatly feared has come upon me, and that which I was afraid of has come unto me."* Job's experience revealed significant truths unknown to his wife, children, relatives, or closest friends.

Probably, no one before or after *Job* ever cursed their birthday and everything surrounding that day with such venom. God orchestrated the calamities to reveal and draw out everything buried in *Job's* heart, breaking his attachments to preserve his life.

Once the spirit of fear, worry, pretense, and death was revealed, *Job* truthfully repented, was delivered, and set free. For the first time, *Job* was free to worship God in spirit and truth.

God's ultimate goal is to work with us to fulfill our covenant agreement with Him. Everything that holds us bound, even if it is unknown to anyone else, must be drawn out and revealed to us. This revelation sets us free, enabling us to know the true and living God and worship Him in spirit and truth. In this truth lies our deliverance, liberty, and freedom in life.

"Human Experience: An Inconvenient Truth" goes beyond heaven and hell. Heaven or hell is not the end of God's eternal purpose. In the end, God will *fill all in all* as He was before the beginning of His creations. It strikes at the root of all believers' faith. The mystery of human experience tests our commitment to God, just as *Job* was tested. It challenges us to serve, love, praise, worship Him, and be committed to His Word daily for all the days of our lives. Even when everything around us is shaken to its foundation, may our roots in God stand firm!

The Significance of Each Day

Each day's break is not as ordinary as most would think. For instance, consider 'July 1st, 2022.' It is not just the first day of July 2022, but a day impregnated with every assignment meant for all people on Earth. This day delivers quintuplets:

1. The Day: *07.01.2022*

2. The Day of the Week: *Friday*

3. The Month: *July*

4. The 3rd Quarter: *July to September*

5. The remaining half of 2022: *July to December*

These deliverables make this day more significant than any other day for the rest of 2022 in the spiritual scheme of God's prophetic calendar. The angels and Satan, along with human agents, execute the assignments for each day according to our covenant with God.

The angels and Satan are acutely aware of the enormity of each day's significance, but most of us probably aren't. *Job's* utterances revealed something about the 'day' of his birth. It revealed his state of mind during his experience. Many of us may not curse the day we were born, but we certainly have questions about it, such as *"Why was I even born into this world with all these troubles?"* At such a time, nothing makes human sense.

In our grand human existence, we are often confronted with life's inconvenient truths—the realities we would rather not face, the mysteries we would rather not unravel. These paradoxes confound us; the contradictions bewilder us; and the ambiguities perplex us. Yet it is in the heart of these inconvenient truths that we find the essence of our human experience.

Transcending life's inconvenient truths is not about denying or running away from them. It is about acknowledging, understanding, and learning from them. It is about embracing the complexity of life, the uncertainty of existence, and its unpredictability from human understanding. It is about finding meaning amid chaos, hope in despair, and light during darkness. Transcendence is a journey of growth, evolution, and transformation—a path of self-discovery, self-awareness, and self-realization. It is a quest for truth, wisdom, knowledge, and understanding of our God.

Transcending life's inconvenient truths involves seeing beyond the surface, looking beyond the obvious, and thinking beyond the conventional. It is about questioning the status quo, challenging norms, and defying standards. It is about breaking chains of conformity, shattering walls of complacency, and transcending boundaries of mediocrity.

In the end, transcending life's inconvenient truths is about living a life of authenticity, integrity, and sincerity—a life of purpose, passion, and potential. It is about living with courage, resilience, and perseverance. It is about thriving, not just surviving; flourishing, not just existing; and becoming, not just being.

CHAPTER 5

The Invisible Hand

"Before God fulfills His Promises, He will TEST you. He will make sure that you believe in His Faithfulness alone." - Alice Hope Wagner, writer

Satan proceeds to implement his second assignment from God, targeting Job's health as permitted by the Omniscient One.

Job's New Trials

Job is still reeling from the loss of his children, sheep, camels, oxen, donkeys, and other possessions. He has no idea what his wife is thinking about his overwhelming ordeal. But Satan wastes no time. Suddenly, *Job* is struck with horrible boils and sores, from the crown of his head to the soles of his feet. In agony, he cries out, "My God, my God, what is going on, and why have you forsaken me?"

Sound familiar? Neither age nor wisdom could prepare him for this. This final jolt shakes *Job* to the core of his being, revealing the divine truth and eternal reality of good and evil. *Job*, not knowing what else to do, wishes to die. Life seems to offer nothing more. A thorough examination of God's orchestration involving Satan unveils the day's destiny for *Job* and his family, according to their agreements. This inconvenient truth stings if left unrevealed and misunderstood.

In times of utter hopelessness and desperate need, many of us might consider suicide to end our misery. *Job* wished for the same. He breaks a piece of pottery to scrape his skin and covers himself with ashes to alleviate the agonizing pain. The air in his home fills with a putrefying odor from his body. By this time, Job's wife can no longer handle the pressure of their recent calamities.

Job's Wife Loses Hope

Job's wife enters the bedroom, squeezing her nose to avoid the full intensity of the odor. She laments, "Are you still trying to be godly? Are you still maintaining your integrity and faithfulness to God? Look at what He has done to us, especially you. Why not curse Him and die? I'm moving on with my life. I don't want to sit here, nurse you, and watch you decay. I might be next to be afflicted. I'm terrified. Is this how God shows His love?" From the look on her face, she is terrified. It would be abnormal not to be. Her life, as she knew it, was fast crumbling all around her.

Job manages to lift his head and look at his wife, tears rolling down his cheeks. "You are talking like a heathen, callous, foolish woman. Are we to receive only blessings from God and never anything unpleasant? Go on and enjoy your life. I will maintain my faith and trust in the Lord, no matter my circumstances. He is still my God."

To raise ten children together and guide them to independence, Mr. and Mrs. Job must have shared a considerable bond. So, what changed? Life has a way of pushing us to the brink. Job's wife is no exception. She swings open the bedroom door and slams it behind her out of frustration and anger. Mrs. Job is human, too. She leaves the house with her friends, planning to distract herself. A couple of friends, worried about Mrs. Job, ask, "Is he okay? What has become of him after all these calamities?"

'I don't understand what's going on anymore,' she responds. '*Why* are we going through all this after serving God for so long? Where is God's protection that my husband often boasts about? I'm baffled. Anyway, let's go before I lose my sanity. I have only one life to live, and I must live it up.'

Mrs. Job's friends likely convinced her to take some time out after losing all her children and possessions. It might be best for her to gather her thoughts away from that environment. Within minutes, they hurry off the estate and head to the town square. Mrs. Job continues, 'Based on his condition, there is no hope. There's no way he's going to survive this. Ladies, it is that bad and scary.' From this point on, no further comment about *Job* is heard from his wife. *Job* is left on his own, in obscurity.

Job's Steadfast Faith

For *Job*, worshiping God, praying, fasting, and living righteously have always been his way of life. Despite everything, *Job* remains steadfast. No amount of caution, planning, or preparation could have prevented this divine appointment. Nobody desires to suffer, so we plan our lives to avoid it. We strive for good education, good jobs/careers, and well-planned lives. However, suffering finds its way into our lives despite our efforts. Such experiences lead us to ask why, especially after investing so much time and effort into different endeavors.

It is the revelation by the Holy Spirit that opens our understanding of our covenant with our heavenly Father. This revelation helps us reconcile our *'whys.'* The sufferings represent the cup we must drink as a pathway to the glory set before us. We must all drink from the cup of our individual *Job experience* to fulfill our purpose on earth. We may never ascertain the precise duration of *Job's* ordeal—whether it lasted days, weeks, months, or even years. Nonetheless, his entire experience is chronicled within the forty-two chapters of the Book of Job.

We can draw from the experience of another faithful servant of God: Abraham. Known as God's friend, Abraham's experience lasted at least seventy-five years before his divine visitation and encounter with God. It was then that the promise to bless him and make him a great nation was revealed.

Neither *Job* nor Abraham remembered their agreements, and we don't remember ours either. But God is faithful to fulfill His part of the covenant with us. What compelled Judas to betray Jesus? The answer lies in the behind-the-scenes conversations between God Almighty and Satan, similar to those in the first two chapters of the Book of Job. The same answer compelled Satan to execute his assignments on *Job* and his family. The same answer was responsible for why the serpent beguiled Eve, Cain killing Abel, and many other events throughout history.

This same driving force was behind Pharaoh's hardened heart, Haman's determination to eliminate the Jews, and Herod's decree to kill all infants under two years old. It fueled Hitler's extermination of six million Jews and Osama bin Laden's orchestration of the 9/11 attacks. This powerful force is still at work today, pushing leaders like Putin to invade Ukraine and causing global suffering. It is the power of the mystery of iniquity.

The Purpose of Our Trials

The pattern Son, Jesus, faced this force until His final words, *"It is finished."* All the fine print in our covenant agreements with our Father must be perfectly executed. *Why?* Because of the glory set before us. Our perfection depends on it, and the glory awaiting us is indescribable, beyond what any eyes have seen or ears have heard. No human mind can comprehend it either.

Achieving mastery in life's journey requires a deep understanding of life's inconvenient truths. It demands a profound understanding of human experience, its complexities, and its mysteries. This journey towards mastery is not linear but a labyrinth of experiences, each offering unique lessons. It requires resilience, patience, and an unwavering commitment to personal growth. It is about embracing life's challenges—the failures, disappointments, and inconvenient truths—as stepping stones toward self-improvement and self-discovery.

The mystery of human experience lies in its unpredictability. It is filled with unexpected twists, highs, lows, joys, and sorrows. Navigating these complexities deepens our understanding of ourselves, the world, and, importantly, our God! Achieving mastery in life's journey involves more than acquiring knowledge or skills. It is about cultivating wisdom, developing emotional intelligence, and fostering empathy and compassion. It is about navigating life's complexities with grace, humility, and resilience.

In the end, the journey towards mastery is lifelong. It challenges us to confront life's inconvenient truths, embrace human experience, and strive for a deeper understanding of ourselves and the world. This journey is the essence of life itself.

CHAPTER 6

Faithfulness and Trust

"Your faithfulness makes you trustworthy to God." - Edwin Louis Cole, author

"God has a purpose behind every problem. He uses circumstances to develop our character." - Rick Warren, author

Job's Faithful Friends

Shortly after Job is afflicted with boils and sores, three men about his age approach his estate. A fourth man, who looks much younger, follows at a distance. They have heard about the calamities that have befallen their friend. These men are Eliphaz, Bildad, Zophar, and Elihu. They come from various parts of the region to support *Job*. His story has become the major news in the land of *Uz* and beyond, though they do not yet grasp its gravity.

As they draw nearer, their identities become clearer. These are *Job's* most trusted friends. Elihu, the youthful figure, maintains a respectable distance from the others. They enter *Job's* home and head straight to the living room, where the front door is ajar. When *Job* hears their voices, he beckons them to come into the bedroom. The men are shocked by what they see. Without uttering a single word, each finds a seat on the floor.

Expressions of Sorrow

Knowing *Job* well, they likely formulated what to say to him before arriving. However, scarcely recognizing him, each person tears his robes, throws his hands in the air, and puts ashes on his head, expressing their sorrow in solidarity with *Job*. They begin to wail loudly to comfort and console him, showing they share his pain. After the wailing ends, silence and agony overpower them for seven days and seven nights. For those seven days and nights, no one in *Job's* bedroom uttered a word. *Job's* friends immediately acknowledge that his suffering and grief are too great for words. Silence seems like the best response. The silence in the room is so deafening that one can hear the buzzing sound of mosquitoes.

Job's Lamentations

Suddenly, the silence breaks. From a place of deep pain, frustration, hopelessness, and agony, with many questions but no answers, *Job* begins to lament. He curses the day he was born, declaring it should be a dark and gloomy day that should not exist in the human calendar. *Job* proclaims, "It would have been better for me to die stillborn than to be delivered by my mother into this world. Let the day of my birth be shrouded in eternal darkness."

Job's friends, who share his mindset, beliefs, and views about God, immediately condemn him. They conclude that God would not punish *Job* if he were as innocent as he claimed. To them, *Job* must have done something wrong to draw God's wrath on his family and possessions. They question *Job* constantly, trying to understand how a just, good, and loving God did not protect him from evil, and to validate his claim as a righteous man who fears God and eschews evil.

The Testing of Faith

The same can be said about us today. If a person is going through their *Job* experience, those around them may question their faith and righteousness. *Job's* friends represent the voices that question, judge, and challenge our faith during trials. Their condemnation stems from a misunderstanding of God's purpose and ways.

Faithfulness and trust in God do not guarantee a life free from suffering. Instead, they are tested and refined through trials. *Job's* unwavering faith amidst his suffering serves as a powerful example of trust in God's sovereignty and faithfulness. Despite his friends' accusations and his deep anguish, *Job* does not curse God. His faith is tested to its limits, but he remains steadfast.

The Purpose of Trials

God's purpose in allowing trials is multifaceted. They test our faith, refine our character, and deepen our dependence on Him. *Job's* experience reveals that faithfulness to God includes trusting Him even when we do not understand His ways. Our trials serve a greater purpose in God's divine plan, often beyond our comprehension.

As believers, we must recognize that our trials are not punishments but growth opportunities, deeper trust in God, and knowing Him intimately. They are occasions to demonstrate our faithfulness to Him. Like *Job*, we may not always understand why we suffer, but we can trust that God is with us and helping us to recall our covenant with Him. And He is working out *ALL* things for our good and His glory. Such knowledge will be very liberating if we cooperate as co-laborers with God, as our covenant is being executed daily. Each person's covenant is unique, just as no two people have the same DNA or fingerprint.

In our moments of deepest pain and confusion, let us remember *Job's* example. His story teaches us that faithfulness to God is not contingent on our circumstances. It is rooted in our trust in His character and His promises. As we navigate our own *Job* experiences, may we find strength in our faith and trust in God's unchanging love and faithfulness.

The danger and subtlety of morality-based relationships with God are that we may not know God beyond the blessing stage in our work with Him. It means knowing God just enough to get our needs and wants met, and anything beyond that level that presents trials and challenges to our faith becomes unbearable. Only a relationship rooted in the knowledge and understanding of our covenant with the Author and Finisher of our faith before the foundation of all things will give us the peace that surpasses all understanding.

CHAPTER 7

Divine Wisdom

God's Spirit is the Source of Wisdom

"Where then does wisdom come from? And where is the place of understanding?"

The Search for Wisdom

Throughout the ages, humanity has sought wisdom and understanding. The Book of Job delves deeply into this quest, especially in the face of suffering and adversity. *Job's* journey is a testament to the human struggle to comprehend the mysteries of life and the divine purposes behind our experiences.

In his suffering, *Job* asks profound questions about life, justice, and the nature of God. He seeks answers that elude him, wrestling with the seeming contradictions between his faith in a just God and the overwhelming calamities he endures. *Job's* search for wisdom is not merely intellectual; it is deeply personal and existential.

The Role of Divine Wisdom

Divine wisdom is a central theme in the Book of Job. It is portrayed as something beyond human grasp, residing with God alone. The wisdom of God is unfathomable, encompassing the mysteries of creation, the workings of the universe, and the intricate details of our lives. In his "Hymn to Wisdom," *Job* reflects on the elusiveness of true wisdom. He acknowledges that while humans can mine the earth for precious metals and gems, true wisdom cannot be found through human effort. It is hidden from the eyes of all living things and is known only to God.

God's Response to Job

When God finally speaks to *Job* out of the whirlwind, He does not provide the answers *Job* seeks. Instead, God reveals His sovereignty and the vastness of His creation. He asks *Job* a series of rhetorical questions that highlight the limits of human understanding and the greatness of divine wisdom.

God's response underscores that His ways and thoughts are higher than ours. He challenges *Job* to consider the complexities of the natural world—the foundations of the earth, the boundaries of the sea, the constellations in the sky, and the instincts of wild animals. Through this revelation, God reminds *Job* of His omnipotence and the divine wisdom that governs the universe.

Job's Humble Response

Confronted with the majesty and wisdom of God, *Job* responds with humility and repentance. He acknowledges his limitations and his inability to understand the divine purposes behind his suffering. *Job's* confession, "I have uttered what I did not understand, things too wonderful for me, which I did not know," reflects his recognition of the vast gap between human knowledge and divine wisdom.

Job's journey from questioning to humility teaches us that true wisdom begins with the fear of the Lord. It involves acknowledging our limitations and trusting in God's sovereign purposes, even when we do not understand them. *Job's* experience invites us to relinquish our need for answers and embrace a posture of trust and reverence before God.

The Gift of Divine Wisdom

While divine wisdom is beyond human attainment, God graciously offers us glimpses of it through His Word and Spirit. God reveals His character, His promises, and His redemptive plan for humanity. The Holy Spirit guides us into all truth, helping us discern God's will and apply His wisdom to our lives.

We are called to seek wisdom through prayer, study of Scripture, and reliance on the Holy Spirit. "If any of you lacks wisdom, let him ask of God, who gives to all generously and without reproach, and it will be given to him." God delights in granting wisdom to those who earnestly seek it, recognizing our dependence on Him.

Living in the Light of Divine Wisdom

Living in light of divine wisdom involves aligning our lives with God's purposes and values. It requires us to prioritize His kingdom, seek His righteousness, and trust His providence. Divine wisdom shapes our decisions, influences our relationships, and guides our actions. In practical terms, living by divine wisdom means cultivating a heart of humility, a spirit of gratitude, and a life of obedience. It calls us to love others sacrificially, serve with integrity, and pursue justice and mercy. It challenges us to walk by faith, not by sight, trusting that God's wisdom is at work in every aspect of our lives.

The journey of seeking and embracing divine wisdom is transformative. It deepens our relationship with God, enriches our understanding of His ways, and equips us to navigate life's challenges with grace and confidence. As we grow in wisdom, we reflect the character of Christ and bear witness to His truth in a world that desperately needs it. Let us, like *Job*, humbly submit to the divine wisdom of our Creator. In doing so, we find peace in His sovereignty, joy in His presence, and hope in His promises. May our lives be a testament to the power and beauty of living by divine wisdom.

The concept of God as the Omniscient is not merely an abstract theological construct but a profound truth that has profound implications for our understanding of the human experience. It suggests that there is a divine plan, a cosmic blueprint, that guides the course of our lives. This plan, in its infinite wisdom, is beyond our limited human understanding.

We may not always comprehend the reasons behind our trials and tribulations, but we can find solace in the belief that they are part of a larger, divine plan. God's omniscience also underscores the limitations of human knowledge. Despite our scientific advancements and intellectual prowess, there is a realm of understanding that remains forever beyond our grasp.

This is not a cause for despair, but rather a humbling reminder of our place in the grand scheme of things. It invites us to approach life with humility and reverence, acknowledging the mystery and wonder that permeates our existence. The mystery of human experience, then, is not a puzzle to be solved but a divine mystery to be lived. It is an invitation to surrender to the wisdom of the divine, to trust in the omniscience of God, and to embrace the inconvenient truth that our understanding will always be limited. In doing so, we open ourselves to a deeper, more profound experience of life, one that is imbued with a sense of awe, wonder, and reverence.

To see God's wisdom working out His purpose from a gross standpoint can be too complex for the natural mind's comprehension. Attempting to understand it in finer detail may be better for us humans. However, this can be mind-boggling; therefore, we rely on what is relatable to us—specifically, the physical sensations that make sense to humans: touch, smell, sight, taste, and hearing. Though *Job's* three friends struggled at best to provide answers to their friend's experience, all their pearls of wisdom combined fell short.

Elihu, the youngest of *Job's* friends, whose name is not mentioned at the beginning among the friends visiting *Job*, has had enough. He is terribly angry with *Job* and his three older friends. He can no longer contain his patience. His ears are full now. He must let the other three have a piece of his mind about their ignorance and stupidity regarding God's sovereignty and purpose. It's as if Elihu takes a peek into the mind of God and lets his indignation, out of frustration for his older friends, flow from his lips, holding nothing back. He explodes with pent-up anger and vows to tell the truth.

He begins by refuting the allegations and giving advice to the older three friends who have leveled against *Job* what they did not understand. Elihu continues to speak in defense of God. "I am young," he declares, "but it is not only the old who are wise. Please listen to my words. It is unthinkable for God to do wrong. God shows no partiality, and Job speaks like the wicked, not the righteous. What does *Job's* righteousness give to God, the possessor of all things? He needs nothing from anyone. Even if He does, how would you know? His voice is like thunder at its peak. By His breath alone, water freezes and forms ice. No one dares to challenge His power."

"Your highest human wisdom and knowledge equate to nothing more than the highest foolishness with God. Then, what makes any of you think the Almighty derives a badge of honor or benefits from *Job's* experience? Do you realize that the whole of creation is like a classroom for God? He uses the birds and beasts to teach us, humans, some science lessons."

Elihu even calls *Job* and his 'wiser' friends an ignoramus bunch in so many ways—thundering clouds without rain. The three older friends are in awe and can hardly believe what they are hearing from young Elihu. Eliphaz, Bildad, and Zophar are subject matter experts in the art of blabbing and lack sensitivity and knowledge of *Job's* background. *Job* is also more confused about his three friends, whom he always considered his wisest friends. After listening to Elihu, *Job* and his three friends are hoping that God will not speak anymore. The friends are beginning to realize that they do not have a deep understanding of God and are wondering what they have been talking about throughout their counsels to Job.

Who can blame them? Consider this. Can the blind lead the blind? Each of the three friends, claiming to be experts, counseled their grieving friend based on their level of understanding and knowledge of God. Their counsel lacked God's divine purpose. When none of the friends could remind Job of his foreknowledge about his experience, God had to step in and do it Himself. Most of the time, the ones who appear to know it all usually aren't those who provide solutions to our problems. God will use the insignificant people to reveal Himself and confound man's wisdom, as contrasted between *Job's* three wise friends and Elihu.

When God interrupts our plans, it is because He wants to steer us back to our divine covenant agreement to fulfill His purpose. We agreed to that plan and signed on the dotted line with the hosts of heaven as witnesses. If we are wise, we will pause and seek out why our plan is not working. As the Spirit of God begins to awaken our consciousness and align our plans with our divine covenant agreement, meaningful changes toward a clear path begin to emerge. Until this happens, we cannot make any headway in our human experience. *Job* and his friends are no different.

Our lack of divine guidance, wisdom, and revelation about our covenant leads to frustrations and disappointments in life. Only divine insight and understanding can bring us to the remembrance of our original agreement with our heavenly Father. In the earthly realm, we must come to work out His or our plan that brings Him pleasure and glory.

When we are in alignment with our divine covenant, our lives take on a purposeful and entirely different meaning. We must continue to ask Him for that wisdom and revelation that enable us to comprehend and connect the dots from our past to our present. Connecting the dots wisely becomes the candle that lights our pathway. The light that leads us further toward our eternal destiny is in God, the Creator and the source of all things, visible and invisible.

CHAPTER 8

All Powerful

"The artist must be in his work as God is in creation, invisible and all-powerful; one must sense him everywhere but never see him."- Gustave Flaubert, a French novelist

"The all-powerful is he who does not wait but makes others wait." - Pierre Bordieu, a French sociologist

"Behold, God is mighty, but despises no one; He is mighty in strength of understanding."

The Omnipotence of God

The omnipotence of God is a central theme in the Book of *Job*. Throughout his trials, *Job* is reminded of God's supreme power and authority over all creation. This realization becomes a source of comfort and strength for *Job* as he grapples with his suffering and seeks to understand God's purposes.

God's omnipotence means that He is all-powerful and capable of accomplishing anything He wills. There is nothing too hard for Him, no challenge too great, and no situation beyond His control. This divine attribute assures us that God is fully able to fulfill His promises and bring His plans to fruition.

God's Power in Creation

One of the most profound demonstrations of God's power is seen in the creation. The universe, with its vast galaxies, intricate ecosystems, and complex life forms, testifies to the might and wisdom of the Creator. God uses the wonders of creation to illustrate His power and challenge *Job's* understanding.

God asks Job questions that highlight the limitations of human knowledge and the greatness of His creative power. "Where were you when I laid the foundation of the earth? Tell me, if you have understanding." These questions emphasize that God's power is immense and incomprehensible to finite human minds. But we were all in Him.

God's Power in Sustaining Life

God's omnipotence is also evident in His sustaining power. He upholds the universe by the word of His power, ensuring that everything functions according to His divine order. The sun rises and sets, the seasons change, and life continues because God sustains it all.

Elihu acknowledges God's sustaining power: "If He should set His heart on it, if He should gather to Himself His Spirit and His breath, all flesh would perish together, and man would return to dust." This passage reminds us that our very existence depends on God's ongoing provision and care.

God's Power in Human Affairs

God's power is not limited to the natural world; it extends to human affairs. He orchestrates events, raises leaders, and directs the course of history according to His sovereign will. Throughout history, we have seen examples of God's intervention in the lives of individuals and nations, demonstrating His control over human destiny. Any human attempt to usurp God's authority and power is at our peril.

For instance, King Nebuchadnezzar turned into a beast and ate grass like an ox for seven years, until he learned his lesson. That experience led him to declare that it is God who is over the affairs of men and rules over the armies of heaven, and no one dares ask Him what He is doing.

In the story of *Job*, God's power is evident in the permission He grants Satan to test *Job*. While God allows *Job* to undergo severe trials, He sets boundaries that Satan cannot cross. This demonstrates that even in our suffering, God remains in control, and His purposes will ultimately prevail.

The Purpose of God's Power

The purpose of God's power is not to instill fear or dominate, but to accomplish His good and perfect will. God's power is always exercised by His character—His love, justice, mercy, and faithfulness. He uses His power to redeem, restore, and bring about His kingdom on earth.

In *Job's* story, we see that God's power ultimately leads to *Job's* restoration and blessing. After *Job* humbles himself and acknowledges God's sovereignty, God restores his fortunes and blesses him with twice as much as he had before. This outcome illustrates that God's power is redemptive and restorative, bringing hope and healing to those who trust in Him.

Trusting in God's Power

As believers, we are called to trust in God's omnipotence, even when we do not understand His ways. Trusting in God's power means recognizing that He is in control, that He is working all things for our good, and that His plans cannot be thwarted. In times of trial and uncertainty, we can find comfort in knowing that God is all-powerful. His strength sustains us, His wisdom guides us, and His love surrounds us. When we feel weak and helpless, we can rely on His power to carry us through.

Living in the Light of God's Power

Living in the light of God's power involves acknowledging His sovereignty in every area of our lives. It means surrendering our fears, worries, and plans to Him, trusting that He can do immeasurably far more than we can ever ask or imagine. Practically, this involves a posture of humility and dependence on God. We seek His guidance through prayer, align our lives with His Word, and step out in faith, knowing that His power is at work within us. It also means recognizing that God's power is made perfect in our weakness. When we are weak, He is strong, and His grace is sufficient for us.

The omnipotence of God is a source of great comfort and strength for believers. It reassures us that God is in control, that He can fulfill His promises, and that His purposes will ultimately prevail. As we trust in His power, we can face life's challenges with confidence, knowing that our all-powerful God is with us, sustaining us, and working all things for our good.

Let us, like *Job*, humbly submit to the omnipotence of our Creator. In doing so, we find peace in His sovereignty, strength in His power, and hope in His promises. May our lives be a testament to the greatness and goodness of our all-powerful God.

Why did it take *Job* so long to see what the Almighty was trying to communicate to him? The answer lies in the inconvenient truth that our human experience is intricately connected to our divine covenant with God. We do not see it or know it until God reveals it to us. To see and accept that truth requires the grace of God and a clear revelation from His Spirit within us. He had to reveal it to *Job* through the whirlwind, not the still voice.

The Spirit of God manifested in the whirlwind to reveal Himself to *Job*. By appearing as a whirlwind to have an encounter with *Job*, God chose a medium that, without a doubt, would convince *Job* and his friends of His powerful presence. That was the first and only record of *Job* having a one-on-one experience with God. God will make Himself known to us by any means necessary to fulfill His purpose with us, in us, and to His glory.

God finally answers *Job* in the eye of a violent whirlwind. For *Job*, it took the sound of the violent wind sweeping through *Uz* like a tornado capable of causing seismic catastrophic damage to the land to see and believe. Out of the violent whirlwind thundered the voice of God. The voice of power, the voice of glory, and the voice of His Majesty. God affirmed Elihu's testimony after all.

Job then repented and was restored. When our dealings with the Almighty are based on morality and religiosity, the spirit of religion and our earthly-bound mindset blind us from seeing the place of our origin and what transpired between us and our Father in heaven. That was also what *Job* had to struggle with. Until we come to the knowledge of the truth about our covenant with our heavenly Father, we cannot, even in a thousand years, understand the *'whys'* of our experience in life.

God was demanding straight answers to His series of questions spanning from the creation of the heavens and the earth to the creatures, large and small. God reminds *Job* that he was there with Him and was a participant in the entire creation process. Everything God was saying began to resonate with *Job* and bore witness within his spirit. When God said, "Let us make man in our image, and after our likeness," *Job* was part of the *'us,'* and we were part of the *'us'* too in the spirit.

The revelation of our covenant with God also enables us to know our authority and power. We are indeed more than conquerors through His Spirit that dwells in us. We are created to overcome any adversity during our journey through this earthly realm. God also reminded *Job* about this truth when He compared him to the fiercest and strongest creatures.

God compares Job to the two fiercest creatures, Behemoth and Leviathan

It gets to the point that *Job's* victim mentality provokes God to challenge him and compare him with Behemoth and Leviathan. The Lord is telling *Job* that he was formed in his mother's womb for this moment. This is why he was born into the Earth realm. He is not a victim, but a victorious one for a greater purpose than the life he has lived until now.

The Almighty authoritatively commands *Job* to gird himself up like a man. He compares him with the toughest creatures in terms of strength and power—Behemoth and Leviathan. This comparison also characterizes the meanings of *Job's* name, as mentioned earlier: endurance, power, and strength with indefatigability. Behemoth and

Leviathan (characteristics and symbolism) were not just mere creatures or sea monsters.

Ever wondered why God, whose every word matters a great deal, would spend half of a chapter on Behemoth and the next entire chapter on Leviathan in His dialogue with *Job*? These characterizations symbolize *Job's* power and our power: endurance, strength, fierceness, and so on. These are the Omnipotent One's characteristics that were inherent in *Job* and all humans created in His image. Absolutely nothing has the power to defeat us except if our heavenly Father permits it, and He only permits what is in our covenant with Him.

Why would the Omnipotent compare *Job* to Behemoth and Leviathan? God declared that Behemoth "is the chief of the ways of God" and fears nothing. And for Leviathan, the Almighty said, "Anyone who dares to pick up a fight with him will regret it and will not live to remember it" because of his fierce nature.

Job possessed these same characteristics through his authority and as God's heir and joint heir with Christ. With this knowledge in our focus, there is nothing we do not have the power and authority to overcome. No wonder God kept drilling *Job* with those 40 questions and demanding answers from him. The same questions are being presented to us during the *'Job experience'* seasons of our lives.

As God's voice echoes from the eye of the whirlwind, *Job* forgets about his condition and pays close attention to every word he hears from the whirlwind. *Job* finally snaps out of his miserable self-pity party. *Job* should have remembered his foreknowledge of this experience that is now unfolding in the physical realm because *Job* was an ancient son of God. His experience was not a mere coincidence. To the natural mind, *Job's* ordeal still sounds like a mystery man's experience being displayed in a theatrical act.

> *"Gird up now thy loins like a man, I will demand of thee*
> *and answer thou me… Behold everyone proud and abase*
> *him. Look on everyone that is proud and bring him low.*
> *Thread down the wicked in their place, hide them together*
> *in the dust and bind their faces in secret. Thy own right*
> *hand can save thee."*

These words were God's admonition to *Job*. God was not interested in *Job's* self-pity or emotions; Job's covenant agreement must be fulfilled. Yes, He does store our tears in a bottle, and none goes to waste. But no volume of our tears would change our covenant agreement with Him. Why? Because His glory, which He will share with no man, depends on our double portion blessing. Consequently, we too are bound by our covenant agreement with God. His glorious promise to us, the manifestation of the sons of God, and the liberation of all creation are at stake.

God was saying to *Job*, 'Don't you recall who you are and how you were with Me among the sons of God before and during the creation of all things? Of course, you agreed to it all. None of your experiences have been imposed on you by Me.'

And, yes, *Job* agreed to it because his glorious double-portion blessing, in the end, was worth his experience. Ah, we too agreed to every bit of our *'Job' experience,* though it may not be clear or seem like a horrible nightmare. If only we could see it and believe it.

God continues with His demand for answers from *Job.* Like us, of course, with so many years gone by, from physical birth to adulthood, how could *Job* remember? *Job* has completely forgotten everything about his covenant. It can only be seen when we take the time to understand the history of others who have come and gone before us.

It is a higher existence for man than this cursed state we find ourselves in through physical birth and mortal consciousness. It reveals to us our position in the presence of God: Man with the incorruptible life of God available to him! Man as master and lord over all things! Man living above sin, sickness, pain, limitation, or death!

This is our glorious portion at the end, after our double portion blessing here on earth, and it is worth every experience we can ever go through. The more God speaks, the more *Job's* memory comes alive, and his understanding of what he has been experiencing is increasing. *Job's* eyes are popping wide open, and he can barely blink for fear of missing something. Without this understanding, life will never make sense. This clarity and understanding reset our faith, assurance, and peace in God.

Job does not remember anymore that before he was conceived, he sat down with the Father of all spirits and the God of all flesh to draw up his covenant agreement before departing from heaven to the earthly realm through the birth process. The Alpha and the Omega, the Omniscient, the Omnipotent, and the Omnipresent One does this to confirm His love toward His children and their liberty to partake freely with Him in all things.

Preparation for Our Experience

To the earth, we must come to be perfected. The earth is the arena, our *Uz*, if you will, where we are trained and made complete to know good and evil, an attribute of our heavenly Father, the Omniscient One. All our battles or experiences go on in our earth-body first at different levels, like a kingdom in conflict within, before being made manifest to the outside world around us. The understanding of our covenant gives us the wisdom to see beyond the natural realm into the spiritual. That understanding allows us to know when the curtain starts to close here on earth, thus preparing us for our journey back home.

Our God is the author of order, not confusion. If *Job* had remembered, he would have known that from our beginning, God ensured we carefully went over our covenant, or terms and conditions, if you will, as the departure date to earth drew near. The final covenant must be thoroughly reviewed for clarity of purpose and to provide an opportunity to make amendments where necessary. It was the covenant for our earthly journey, with eternal glory as the goal. Once reviewed, finalized, and signed by both parties—by us and our heavenly Father—it was then sealed as our books in heaven's library.

Therefore, our agreement is duly documented in our book, stored in heaven. That is the vault where the mystery of our human experience is kept from all eyes, including the angels. The book becomes our volume in heaven. But like all men and women on earth, *Job* does not remember it, and neither do we.

With this understanding, *Job* realized that the Almighty and the Omnipotent One had already equipped him with all that he needed to overcome in his experience. With this revelation, he abhorred himself and pleaded with God for mercy and forgiveness. God was making *Job* more aware of himself, his authority, and his power relative to his experience. *Job* was as old as the Ancient of Days, but he did not even know it. No question! For in Him we live, move, and have our being. We have always been in Him and with Him throughout all generations—past, present, and future.

Acknowledging Our Experience

Job acknowledges and worships God for His power and sovereignty over all the universe, visible and invisible. He repents in dust and ashes. It is evident that Job is coming full circle, after his experience, to know good and evil like all sons of God, whom He loves, must know. The Elohim's primordial desire is that we know Him and reflect His image. The mystery of our human experience achieves that purpose for God and us.

Job's experience has an appointed time in heaven, according to God's prophetic calendar. And we have our appointed time to go through our *Job's* experience according to an agreed schedule in heaven before the foundation of all things. Without this experience, *Job* would never have known the ministry of God's left hand. To know God, the right-hand ministry must be balanced with the left-hand ministry to fulfill His divine purpose.

Job agreed to his experience just as the pattern Son agreed to go to the cross to fulfill His destiny in God's all-encompassing prophetic plan and covenant agreement, signed before the foundation of all things. The pattern Son, Jesus, stated it very clearly as follows: "For this purpose, I came into the world to fulfill that which was written of me in the volume of the book, and I have come to do your will, O God." Yes, it is true in the scriptures, but it is also true in the volume of His book in heaven.

Judge the author by the Spirit of God. If what you are reading or hearing is the truth and bears witness within your spirit, then trust that it is true. The spirit of Christ in you will have an affinity for what you are reading or hearing. If what the author is saying does not bear witness to your spirit or have an affinity with the Spirit of God in you, discard it.

Alignment Through Our Experience

Thus, when God began to speak to *Job*, he had to test the spirit. And what *Job* was hearing bore witness, so strong with his spirits, to the extent that he knew indeed that God Almighty was the One speaking to him. Without a doubt, *Job* had no other place to turn or anything else to do but to repent, be healed, and be blessed with a double portion of all that he ever had and lost physically in this earthly realm. *Job's* end speaks more than we can fathom with our natural minds. Only the mind of Christ and revelation from God can help us grasp to some degree what *Job's* experience is communicating to us and all humanity from creation until now.

There exists an omnipotent force, a divine entity, that governs the affairs of men. This entity, often referred to as God, is believed to be the ultimate source of all power and authority and the supreme arbiter of fate and destiny. The concept of an omnipotent God ruling over the affairs of men is not a new one; it has been a cornerstone of many religious and philosophical systems throughout history.

The omnipotent God is often depicted as a benevolent figure, guiding humanity towards righteousness and justice. However, this divine entity is also seen as a stern judge, meting out punishment to those who stray from the path of virtue. The belief in an omnipotent God provides a moral framework for human behavior, instilling a sense of responsibility and accountability in individuals.

Yet the mystery of human experience is such that it often challenges this belief. The existence of suffering and injustice in the world raises questions about the nature of this omnipotent God. If God is all-powerful and benevolent, why does He allow such atrocities to occur? This is the paradox that lies at the heart of our human experience.

The belief in an omnipotent God ruling over the affairs of men is an inconvenient truth for many. It forces us to confront the reality of our existence and grapple with the complexities of morality and justice. It challenges us to seek answers to the most profound questions of life and death, of purpose and meaning. It is a belief that shapes our understanding of the world and our place in it, a belief that continues to influence the course of human history. In the end, He helps us align with His plan as it is revealed through our experience.

CHAPTER 9

Patience and Restoration

The mystery and the dichotomy of life rest in discerning Job's experience.

"The Lord blessed the latter days of Job more than his beginning."

The Turning Point

After a long period of suffering and questioning, the story of *Job* takes a dramatic turn. A significant change occurs when *Job* finally acknowledges God's omnipotence and repents for questioning His ways. This turning point is marked by *Job's* humble submission and renewed trust in God.

God never blamed him because he was sincere and simply innocently ignorant, coupled with his lost memory. Our sincere anger, out of a pure heart, toward God our Father in the days of our ignorance is not an offense in His estimation of us. He winks at such.

To that end, *Job's* experience was not about his patience, as may have been commonly portrayed. Rather, more appropriately, it was about the patience of God. With God's knowledge of all things, the Omniscient One had to patiently wait until Job and his friends had exhausted all human wisdom and understanding.

Job's Repentance

Job's journey of suffering culminates in a moment of profound humility. *Job* responds to God's revelation with deep repentance: "I know that You can do all things and that no purpose of Yours can be thwarted... I had heard of You by the hearing of the ear, but now my eye sees You; therefore, I despise myself and repent in dust and ashes." *Job's* confession signifies a deeper understanding of God's sovereignty and human limitations. He moves from questioning God to trusting Him completely, even without having all the answers. *Job's* memory, wisdom, understanding, and power are recovered or rediscovered.

Job's experience reveals the truth about his heart. And his heart must be tested and restored to seek and reflect God's heart and nature. It reveals Job to *Job*. It reveals *Job* to his four friends. Albeit this is the *Job* that God has been waiting to see manifest. Yes, it reveals the missteps and faults of Job's older and 'wiser friends,' Eliphaz, Bildad, and Zophar. This is the *Job* that not even his wife or his children knew; only the Omniscient One knew. We do not know ourselves until God reveals us to us—by showing the house to the house.

The Role of Intercession

After *Job* was stripped of his wealth, possessions, health, and immediate family, except his wife, it is important to note that all through the extended dialog between God and *Job*, God never told him the reason He permitted Satan to go after him. Neither did God reveal to him who initiated or orchestrated all his calamities. But no preparation would have prevented his experience. It elevated *Job* to a broader intercessor role beyond his family.

Another pivotal aspect of *Job's* restoration is his intercession for his friends. Despite their harsh accusations and lack of empathy, *Job* prays for them at God's command. God instructs *Job's* friends to offer sacrifices and tells *Job* to pray for them, promising to accept Job's prayer and not deal with them according to their folly. *Job's* willingness to forgive and intercede for his friends demonstrates his obedience and compassion as key factors in his restoration.

The Restoration of Job

Following *Job's* repentance and intercession, God restores his fortunes. The restoration is comprehensive, touching every aspect of *Job's* life:

- *Material Wealth: Job's* wealth is doubled. God blesses him with more livestock and possessions than he had before his trials. This material blessing signifies God's favor and the restoration of *Job's* status and prosperity.

- *Family: Job* is blessed with more children—seven sons and three daughters. His daughters are noted for their beauty, and *Job* ensures they receive an inheritance alongside their brothers, a significant gesture of equality and love.

- *Longevity: Job* lived 140 more years, witnessing four generations of his descendants. His long life is a testament to God's blessing and a reward for his faithfulness.

Lessons from Job's Restoration and Broader Implications

Job's restoration offers several profound lessons for believers:

1. God's Sovereignty: The story reaffirms that God is sovereign, and His purposes are beyond our understanding. Even in suffering, God's plans are good and ultimately lead to restoration and blessing.

2. *Repentance and Humility:* True wisdom begins with humility before God. *Job's* repentance opens the door to restoration, teaching us the importance of humbling ourselves and trusting God's wisdom.

3. *Intercession and Forgiveness: Job's* prayer for his friends highlights the power of intercession and forgiveness. By praying for those who wronged him, *Job* demonstrates the heart of God's love and compassion.

4. *Faithfulness Rewarded:* God honors *Job's* faithfulness and trust. Despite his trials, *Job's* steadfast faith leads to a greater blessing. This encourages believers to remain faithful, knowing that God sees and rewards our faithfulness.

Job's restoration is not just a personal victory; it has broader implications for understanding God's character and His dealings with humanity. It illustrates that God's discipline is meant for our growth and ultimate good. It shows that suffering is not the end of the story but a chapter in the larger narrative of God's redemptive work.

Applying Job's Lessons to Our Lives

As we reflect on *Job's* restoration, we can draw strength and encouragement for our own lives. Here are practical ways to apply these lessons:

- *Trust in God's Sovereignty:* In times of suffering and uncertainty, remember that God is in control. His plans for us are good, and He works all things together for our good.

- *Practice Humility and Repentance:* Cultivate a heart of humility, recognizing our limitations and God's infinite wisdom. When we falter, we repent and turn back to God, trusting in His mercy and grace.

- *Forgive and Intercede:* Follow *Job's* example by forgiving those who wrong us and praying for them. This reflects God's love and opens the door to healing and restoration in relationships.

- *Remain Faithful:* Stay steadfast in your faith, even when facing trials. Trust that God rewards faithfulness and will bring restoration in His perfect timing.

Naturally, we want quick fixes, instant gratification, and immediate results. But God, in His infinite wisdom, knows that true growth and transformation take time. He invites us to embrace this truth, cultivate patience within ourselves, and trust in the process of our evolution. In the mystery of human experience, the patience of God is a beacon of hope, a reminder that we are loved, valued, and believed in, no matter how long our journey takes or how many times we stumble along the way.

The story of *Job* is a powerful testament to the themes of suffering, faith, and restoration. *Job's* journey from loss to restoration highlights God's sovereignty, the importance of humility and repentance, and the power of intercession and forgiveness.

As we navigate our trials, may we hold onto these lessons, trusting that God is faithful and will restore us in time according to our agreement with Him. It encourages us to trust in the all-powerful, all-knowing, and ever-loving God, who works all things for our good. May we, like *Job*, find hope and strength in God's promises, knowing that He is with us through every trial and will lead us to restoration and blessing, and for His glory.

CHAPTER 10

Knowledge and Endurance

The knowledge of our future must be greater to free our present. Unless that happens, our past will continue to control our present.

Endurance and Victory

"Blessed is the one who perseveres under trial because, having stood the test, that person will receive the crown of life that the Lord has promised to those who love him."

The Importance of Endurance

The story of *Job* underscores the vital importance of endurance in the life of a believer. *Job's* journey from affluence through immense suffering and back to restoration exemplifies the power of steadfastness and faith in God's promises. Endurance is our capacity to remain steadfast in the face of adversity, trusting that God is in control and will ultimately bring us through our trials. It is a testimony to our faith and reliance on God's strength rather than our own.

Job's Exemplary Endurance

Job's endurance is remarkable. Despite losing his wealth, health, and children, he never wavers in his faith. *Job's* friends and even his wife question his faithfulness, but he remains resolute, declaring, "Though he slay me, yet will I hope in him."

Job's endurance is not a passive acceptance of suffering but an active, hopeful trust in God's ultimate justice and mercy. He expresses his anguish and questions God, yet he never abandons his faith. This duality of lament and trust is central to enduring faith.

God's Perspective on Endurance

The virtue of endurance encourages believers to "consider it pure joy... whenever you face trials of many kinds, because you know that the testing of your faith produces perseverance. Let perseverance finish its work so that you may be mature and complete, not lacking anything." Furthermore, "suffering produces perseverance; perseverance, character; and character, hope." These words emphasize that endurance is not an end in itself but a pathway to spiritual maturity and deeper hope through our *"Human Experience: An Inconvenient Truth."*

Jesus, the Ultimate Example

Jesus Christ is the ultimate example of endurance and victory. He endured the cross, despising its shame, for the joy set before Him. His endurance in the face of unimaginable suffering paved the way for our salvation and victory over sin and death. His endurance was grounded in His absolute trust in the Father's plan. Even in His darkest hour, He prayed, "Not my will, but yours be done," which was the reason He came to fulfill His agreement on Earth. His example encourages us to endure our trials with the same trust and submission to God's will, being merged with our will.

The Reward of Endurance

The outcome of endurance promises that those who endure will receive a reward. It assures us that "Blessed is the one who perseveres under trial because, having stood the test, that person will receive the crown of life that the Lord has promised to those who love him." *Job's* faith ultimately leads to his restoration. God rewards him by doubling his former possessions, blessing him with more children, and granting him a long and prosperous life. *Job's* story illustrates that God honors and rewards our faith, even if the reward is not immediate and the journey is very inconvenient.

Strengthening Our Faith

Faith can be strengthened through several practices:

1. *Prayer:* Communicating with God through prayer strengthens our relationship with Him and reinforces our trust in His promises.

2. *Scripture:* Studying His word consistently reminds us of God's faithfulness and the countless ways He has fulfilled His promises throughout history.

3. *Fellowship:* Surrounding ourselves with other believers provides encouragement and support, helping us to remain steadfast in our faith.

4. *Worship:* Worshiping God, whether through song, service, or daily obedience, deepens our connection with Him and reinforces our faith.

Living Out Faith

Living out faith involves more than believing in God's promises; it requires acting on them. We must remember that "faith by itself, if it is not accompanied by action, is dead." True faith manifests in our actions, influencing how we live, make decisions, and interact with others. *Job's* life exemplifies this active faith. Despite his suffering, he continues to worship God, intercede for his friends, and live righteously. His faith is evident in his actions, even in the darkest moments.

The story of *Job* is a profound testament to the power of faith. *Job's* unwavering trust in God, despite immense suffering, demonstrates the essence of true faith. His journey teaches us that faith is essential for navigating life's trials and experiencing God's promises. As we reflect on *Job's* story, let us be inspired to cultivate a deep and abiding faith in God. May we trust in His promises, remain steadfast in our trials, and live out our faith in every aspect of our lives. In doing so, we can experience the rewards of faith and the fulfillment of God's ultimate purpose for our lives. He is faithful and will not deny us His promise in our covenant agreement with Him.

Normally, we don't have foreknowledge of the behind-the-scenes events in heaven. Therefore, comprehending how what is manifesting physically on earth is controlled by the spiritual realm does not come naturally. It is only revealed by the Spirit. What anybody thinks or does not think, believes or doesn't believe, makes no difference. God's knowledge of everything that transpires in the world and His perspective on the universe and human experience have a wider scope that is beyond any human comprehension.

The purpose of *Job's* experience was not to determine whether he was perfect. God already declared him perfect and the greatest of all the men of the East. The experience was intended to awaken Job's consciousness and lead him back to his original position as an overcomer in all realms. It shifted Job away from the mindset of 'I-do-good-deeds and I-receive-God's-favor' in his relationship with the Father of all spirits and the God of all flesh. Hence, *"Human Experience:*

An Inconvenient Truth" invites us to understand how *Job's* experience is interconnected with every human experience.

Elihu was the only one among the friends whose spirit confidently discerned the mind of God. Eliphaz, Bildad, Zophar, Job's family, other friends, and all the people of the East who witnessed Job's transformational experience gained more knowledge about the Omnipotent God. How do you see your situation during your mystery of human experience? And how do you see God? Is the mystery of your human experience revealing who you are and who God is to you?

We have forgotten our complete schedule with our heavenly Father

Through the transition of time from God and birth until now, Job has forgotten everything. We have also forgotten everything through the ages. It has indeed been a while since we left our original place of birth in heaven and descended to this world—the earthly realm. It was then that our heavenly Father booked our round-trip flights. He also provided each of us with our boarding passes before we began our journey from Him to Earth.

We shall return to Him as we agreed, according to our confirmed flight ticket details. A few people have become aware that this earth is just a stopover en route to our full-circle journey back home. For those few, when their return date approaches, they will hear the heavenly bell ringing, announcing the time of their departure. They will gather their loved ones to say their final goodbyes before boarding their return flight back home to our Father's bosom.

In Memory of All Our Dear Loved Ones – With a Heavy Heart

As painful as the death of Dr. Myles Monroe and his beloved wife by plane crash was to those who knew him, it was his covenant agreement with the Father that stipulated how he returned home. What about Kobe Bryant, our beloved NBA star, Dr. Herbert Wigwe, and his beloved wife, General Murtala Muhammed, General Johnson Thomas Aguiyi-Ironsi, and President John F. Kennedy, Dr. Martin Luther King, Jr., and Omodele Ogunrombi ("The Able CNN News Anchor Lady")? The list goes on and includes Judas Iscariot, who betrayed our Lord Jesus Christ; they all exited this earth the way their covenant agreement stipulated for their return to the Father. That is the *Inconvenient Truth* we must see to enable us to know the answers to our "W*hys!*" We recall Mary beholding Jesus on the cross in agony.

Our Views of Birth and Death

Heaven mourns the day we depart from there and rejoices the day we return home. On the contrary, the earth or the world rejoices the day we arrive here (into the world) and mourns the day we depart from here and go back home. For example, how do the servicemen or women deployed on assignment to a foreign land feel when it is time to return home? Sad or happy? Don't they look forward with joyful anticipation as the departure date draws near? "God's ways are not our ways, nor are His thoughts our thoughts."

So must we when it comes time to return home to our original homeland to be reunited with our loved ones (the innumerable company of witnesses) who have been patiently waiting for our arrival back in heaven. One songwriter's lyrics profoundly echo the sublime truth that says, "This world is not my home; I'm just passing through." - Albert E. Brumley (made popular by Jim Reeves).

The dead have no memory, do they? Even the Israelites, while in Egypt, forgot that God clearly told Abraham to 'know of a surety' that his descendants would be strangers and slaves in a foreign land for 400 years. And afterward, they will be delivered and come out with great substance. Why would God not interfere with our human experience? It is the same reason why He did not do anything to intervene during the period that the Israelites were suffering in Egypt. He raised and revealed their deliverer (Moses) only when the time He told Abraham was fulfilled.

If God's encounter with Abraham in the divine vision (like *Job's* whirlwind encounter with God) had not been recorded for us to read, the Israelites' 430 years of suffering experience in Egypt would have remained one of the world's mysteries of all ages. It is important to note that Abraham's vision was God's way of reminding Abraham about their covenant agreement, which He and Abraham signed in Heaven before Abraham departed for the Earth realm. Abraham had forgotten. Furthermore, Joseph's dream; being thrown in the pit and then sold to become Potiphar's slave. He was sent to prison and finally called into Pharaoh's palace as second in command over Egypt. All these were part of the fine print in Abraham's agreement (terms and conditions) with God to fulfill as the father of many nations.

More Witnesses Confirming What We Have Forgotten

God, in His chosen events, has not left us without witnesses to remind us about our agreement. When Esau and Jacob were struggling in Rebecca's womb, she inquired why. The Lord reminded her of her covenant agreement regarding the two nations she was pregnant with. Embedded in her agreement were Esau and Jacob's covenant agreements too. Let's consider how our Lord and Savior reminded Judas, specifically saying, "Whatever thou doest, do quickly," after solemnly telling the whole group, "Verily, verily, I say unto you, that one of you shall betray me." Why? It is very inconvenient to think that our Lord's agreement with His Father's purpose was intricately connected to Judas' agreement.

Angel Gabriel was sent to remind Mary about her agreement concerning the Lord Jesus Christ. Our Lord's agreement to do His will and fulfill His purpose through the cross to redeem God's creation was embedded in Mary's agreement in heaven with God before she was born in the flesh. King David, the man after God's heart, could have done nothing to change the immutable covenant with our Father.

We also fulfill our covenant agreement through our human experiences, no matter how inconvenient. It is for the glory set before us from the foundation of the world. Hence our Lord Jesus said thus: "Your father Abraham rejoiced at the thought of seeing my day; he saw it and was glad." When did Abraham see the day of the Lord Jesus and rejoice? Abraham saw it in his covenant agreement. Lord, forgive us for our lost memory.

God Partakes of His Physical Creation

What does Jesus mean when He says, "Let the dead bury the dead?" He knew that *'living'* according to the earth's reality, which is the opposite of heaven's reality, was *'dead'* according to true or spiritual reality. It's important to note that in Jesus' statement, the 'dead' refers to individuals who are spiritually dead due to not being aware of spiritual reality (born-again of the spirit). That is partially true. But, more so, because they are 'dead' from the day God put Adam (His breath or spirit) into the dust of the ground to form man. I say the following with godly fear and humility: God had to bury a part of Himself in the dust of the ground. Put differently, a part of God had to 'die' to partake of His creativity and the things He had created before forming Adam from the dust of the ground.

Why does life begin with conception? Just as God infused His life or breath into the womb of the earth on the day He formed Adam and enclosed him in the earth-body suit, so does the sperm of the man get infused into the womb of the woman and enclosed in the flesh-body to become a living soul to start the death process on the earth. Man could only live or survive physically on earth by being buried in the dust of the ground. Therefore, Adam (the essence of the life and breath of God) couldn't exist or relate to all the things He created without being buried in the earth and becoming part and parcel of it.

Why do 'Bad' things happen to 'Good' people and vice versa?

Without the knowledge and understanding of Job's experience, birth, life, and death in the spiritual context, we would naturally not grasp what 'good' and 'bad' mean in God's economy. But have you wondered why *dreadful things'* happen to *'good people'* and why misfortune does not discriminate between rich or poor, young or old? It has nothing to do with being good or bad. It is according to our covenant agreements. There is a glorious life that is set before us to inherit, as the pattern Son did when He completed the reason why He came to Earth.

The knowledge of the light of our glorious future, scripted in our covenant with our heavenly Father, must outshine the ignorance of our past till now, to enable us to endure the journey of our present Job experience. That is how the pattern Son endured the death of the cross and obtained the joy and glory that were set before Him. Everything Satan offered Him paled in comparison to that glory. Hence, "Get thee behind me, Satan," was all He needed to dispel every attempt to lure Him.

Everything, from birth and beyond, that has happened, is happening, and will ever happen in our lives, like *Job's* experience, is very carefully and strategically woven into our covenant agreement with our heavenly Father. Therefore, if we cast blame on anyone, it is because we have forgotten.

Unfortunately, our ignorance is no excuse. The fire of our experience has one purpose. It is to burn and remove the dross from our clouded minds. Our Omniscient Father had to use the serpent to make mankind—in Eve, then Adam—eat the fruit of the knowledge of good and evil and die spiritually. By doing so, Jesus had to come and *'die'* and lead mankind back to God again and complete His purpose. Hence, he cried out His final words on the cross, saying, *"It Is Finished."*

The ultimate goal of our experience is that the Almighty God is glorified. It did not look like it then. But had *Job's* four friends known, they would have rejoiced that they had the opportunity to observe and witness his trials, tribulations, and triumphs. *Job* did nothing wrong, just as neither the man who was born blind nor his parents sinned. It was so that God would be glorified after his sight was restored by His Son, our Redeemer, Healer, and Lord and Savior.

Jesus obeyed God in all that He did to the end, but He still suffered through the cross. *Job* obeyed God, loved God, was faithful to God, feared God, and eschewed evil daily, yet he still suffered calamities of immense proportion. Why? Both Jesus and *Job* agreed to their experiences as pathways to inheriting their promises in the end to glorify God.

Jesus prayed, "Father, forgive them, for they know not what they are doing," even while they were hanging Him on the cross. How could He pray for them? He prayed for them only because He remembered

His covenant agreement with His Father. His agreement was constantly His focus in all that He did daily.

How could the thief on Jesus' right hand be saved and be with Jesus in paradise while hanging on his cross? He was a professional robber, a hardened criminal to the core, and at the end of his lifetime, he goes straight from the cross to paradise. And our Lord made him an instant paradise candidate model, worthy of sharing in His glorious paradise. Jesus' declaration and acceptance of the thief display the power of our covenant with our heavenly Father. What a mystery!

But then, have you wondered why God would say, "Jacob, *I love*, but Esau, *I hated*"? *Why?* What did Esau do in his mother's womb that led to: "And the older shall serve the younger," as God told his mother before he was born? What did Cain do to be the one whose sacrifice had to be rejected, but Abel's accepted by God? Apostle Paul reminds us during one of his visits to Corinth: "For God said to Moses, 'I will show mercy to anyone I choose, and I will show compassion to anyone I choose.'" *Why?*

What about "Have I not *chosen* you twelve, and *one* of you *is a devil?*" This is our Savior speaking about Judas Iscariot. What did Judas, one of the Lord's disciples, do to be *chosen* as a devil before he was born? And "those that you gave me I have kept, and none of them is lost, but *the son of perdition*; that *the scripture might be fulfilled*." Finally, "Because it is *given* unto you to know the mysteries of the kingdom of heaven, but to them, it is not given," was the Lord's answer to His disciples enquiring from Him why the non-disciples were not understanding His teachings or parables. Our agreement with our Father is the immutable *Inconvenient Truth* that holds the answer!

Why God Remains Silent

The reason God will not raise a finger and let Satan have his field day, no matter how much we pray, is because our covenant with Him before we arrived on earth trumps all the prayers and fasting, binding and loosening, and declaring. Our prayers and fasting must align with our covenant agreement, or else they amount to unprofitable efforts. As God fulfills His part of the covenant, so must we. Every prayer is answered according to our covenant agreement with our Father's purpose. Our planning, our prayers, our will, and our asking, seeking, and knocking must align with His will—as we agreed!

Job's experience embodied the entirety of God's dealings with humanity; revealing the depths of truth and reality worked out by His Spirit. And no amount of ignorance can excuse the experience. Satan is just a facilitator of the process. In parallel, Satan was in Judas facilitating the process of the pattern Son's experience through the cross back to God, as agreed before the foundation of all things.

The Difference Between Our Lord Jesus Christ and Job

Here is the difference between *Job's* experience and the pattern Son's experience: *Job* could not discern Satan spiritually due to *"lost memory."* Satan could not directly challenge the pattern Son because the pattern Son could discern him spiritually. Therefore, Judas, one of the closest in His nucleus ministry, had to be used to unmistakably identify the Son of Man to the human *'executioners.'*

The identification of the pattern Son had to have zero room for error. That was what He came to fulfill, a task that had to be accomplished because all of creation's history hinged on it. The reconciliation of *All Things* to God! The executioners of the pattern Son, who were shouting, "Crucify Him, crucify Him," like Satan, did not know what they were doing. Everyone who directly or indirectly played a part in the ultimate crucifixion of the pattern Son, from start to finish via the cross, was simply fulfilling his or her purpose in the grand master plan of the Omniscient One. Hence, the cry *'IT IS FINISHED'* revealed the mystery of God's knowledge, wisdom, and ultimate purpose.

CHAPTER 11

Ever Present and Eternal Perspective

"The past has no power over the present moment." - Eckhart Tolle, a German author

Eternal Perspective and Limitations of Temporal View

"So, we fix our eyes not on what is seen, but on what is unseen, since what is seen is temporary, but what is unseen is eternal."

Human beings often view life through a temporal lens, focusing on immediate circumstances, needs, and desires. This perspective is limited and can lead to discouragement and despair, especially during times of suffering. When we are consumed by the present moment, we may fail to see the bigger picture of God's eternal plan.

Job's initial struggle reflects this temporal view. He is overwhelmed by his suffering and questions God's justice and goodness. His friends also share this limited perspective, interpreting *Job's* trials as a result of sin without understanding the greater purposes at play.

Assurance of God's Presence

Throughout *Job's* trials, one constant is the presence of God. Even when *Job* feels abandoned, God is there, listening to his cries and ultimately revealing Himself. This assurance of God's presence is a source of comfort and strength for us as we navigate our trials. King David writes, "Where can I go from your Spirit? Where can I flee from your presence? If I go up to the heavens, you are there; if I make my bed in the depths, you are there. If I rise on the wings of the dawn, if I settle on the far side of the sea, even there your hand will guide me, your right hand will hold me fast." This passage reminds us that God's presence is with us always, guiding and sustaining us.

Shift to Eternal Perspective

An eternal perspective transforms how we view our experiences, especially our trials. It involves seeing beyond the present moment and recognizing that our lives are part of a larger, divine narrative. This perspective acknowledges that our sufferings are temporary, and God's ultimate purposes are eternal.

Paul the Apostle emphasizes this shift, encouraging believers to "not lose heart" because "our light and momentary troubles are achieving for us an eternal glory that far outweighs them all." By fixing our eyes on what is unseen and eternal, we gain strength and hope to endure present hardships. 'God only chastises, scourges, and corrects the children He receives as His own, according to His definite purpose' and their covenant agreement with Him. So, dear child of God, do not faint or grow weary when the Father permits Satan to carry out his ministry of testing you. He allows it for your good and your glory.

Job's Revelation of Eternity

Amidst his suffering, Job makes a profound declaration of faith: "I know that my Redeemer lives and that in the end, he will stand on the earth. And after my skin has been destroyed, *yet in my flesh I will see God; I will see him with my own eyes—I, and not another. How my heart yearns within me!"* This revelation marks a pivotal moment in *Job's* journey. Despite his immediate pain, *Job* looks forward to the ultimate redemption and vindication that will come from God. His focus shifts from his current affliction to the hope of seeing God face-to-face. May we meditate on *Job's* encounter with the Voice of God in the whirlwind.

Hope in Eternal Perspective

Hope is a fundamental component of an eternal perspective. It is the confident expectation that God will fulfill His promises and that our present sufferings will give way to our glory. This hope sustains us through trials and motivates us to persevere in faith and compare our present sufferings to the glory that will be revealed in us. Our dear brother Paul describes creation's eager expectation for the children of

God to be revealed and highlights the hope we have as believers for the redemption of our bodies and the restoration of *all things.*

Living with an Eternal Perspective

Living with an eternal perspective involves several key practices:

1. *Renewing Our Minds:* Regularly immerse yourself in God's Word to align your thoughts with His eternal truths, and to be transformed by the renewing of our minds, enabling us to discern God's will revealed by the Holy Spirit.

2. *Focusing on God's Promises:* Meditate on the promises of God that speak into our lives and circumstances.

3. *Embracing Suffering with Faith:* Recognize that suffering is part of our journey and that it serves a greater purpose in God's plan. Trust that God is using your trials to refine your character and for His glory.

4. *Cultivating Gratitude and Contentment:* Practice gratitude for God's blessings and contentment in His provision. Being content in all circumstances through the strength Christ provides.

5. *Engaging in Kingdom Work:* Invest your time and resources in activities that have eternal significance. Serve others, share the gospel, and contribute to the advancement of God's kingdom.

Impact of Eternal Perspective

An eternal perspective not only transforms our individual lives but also influences our interactions with others. It enables us to offer comfort and encouragement to those who are suffering, reminding them of the hope we have in Christ. It also empowers us to live boldly for God's kingdom, knowing that our labor in the Lord is not in vain. This perspective helps us prioritize what truly matters and align our lives with God's eternal purposes. It shapes our values, decisions, and relationships, leading us to live with greater intentionality and purpose for His grace and His glory.

The story of *Job*, viewed through the lens of an eternal perspective, offers profound insights into the nature of suffering, faith, and hope. Job's journey from despair, pain, agony, confusion, misery, and utter hopelessness to revelation highlights the transformative power of seeing our lives in the context of God's eternal plan foreordained according to His purpose and our agreement with Him. As we cultivate an eternal perspective, we find the strength to endure trials, hope, and motivation to live for God's glory. May our lives reflect the hope and assurance of our eternal inheritance in Christ, and may we encourage others to look beyond their present circumstances to the glorious liberty of those called His royal priests. The hosts of heaven are rooting for us.

CHAPTER 12

Infinite Love and Ultimate Purpose

We cannot fully comprehend the depth of God's love for humanity. His love endures forever.

Understanding God's Ultimate Purpose

The story of *Job* is a profound exploration of human suffering, faith, and divine purpose. Throughout *Job's* trials, we see glimpses of God's ultimate purpose—His desire to shape, refine, and draw us closer to Him. God's ultimate purpose for our lives is not just about temporal blessings but about eternal transformation. He desires to mold us into the image of His Son, Jesus Christ, and to prepare us for an eternity with Him. This process often involves trials and challenges that test and strengthen our faith.

The Refining Process

Just as gold is refined by fire, our character is refined through the trials we endure. *Job's* experience is a powerful illustration of this refining process. His suffering strips away everything he relies on, leaving him with nothing but his faith in God. This process exposes and purifies his heart, leading to a deeper, more genuine relationship with God. The Apostle Peter writes about the purpose of trials: "In all this, you greatly rejoice, though now for a little while you may have had to suffer grief in all kinds of trials. These have come so that the proven genuineness of your faith—of greater worth than gold, which perishes even though refined by fire—may result in praise, glory, and honor when Jesus Christ is revealed" in us.

Conforming to the Image of Christ

God's ultimate purpose is for us to conform to the image of His Son. This transformation involves a radical reorientation of our lives, values, and priorities. It requires us to surrender our will to God and to allow His Spirit to work in us, shaping us into Christ's likeness, reconciling, and healing our short memory.

Job's journey reflects this transformation. Initially, *Job* is a man of great faith and integrity, but his understanding of God is incomplete. Through his trials, *Job* gains a deeper understanding of God's character and sovereignty. His faith is no longer based on his blessings but on a profound trust in God's love and wisdom.

Drawing Closer to God

One of the most significant outcomes of Job's trials is his deeper intimacy with God. Job declares, "My ears had heard of you, but now my eyes have seen you." This intimate knowledge of God is the ultimate goal of our faith journey. God uses our trials to draw us closer to Him. When we face difficulties, we are driven to seek God more earnestly, to depend on Him more completely, and to trust Him more fully. This deepened relationship with God is the greatest reward for our faithfulness and endurance.

Living with Purpose

Understanding God's ultimate purpose gives us a new perspective on our lives and the trials we face. It helps us see beyond our immediate circumstances and focus on the eternal significance of our journey. This perspective empowers us to live with greater purpose and intentionality. They are tools used by the divine Craftsman to chisel us into the individuals we are meant to be. Ask a member of the Marine Corps what it takes to qualify and be called a 'Navy SEAL' or a member of the SEALs.

Living with purpose means aligning our lives with God's will and seeking to fulfill His purposes in everything we do. It involves pursuing spiritual growth, serving others, and sharing the good news of the gospel. It means living each day with the awareness that our lives have eternal significance.

Our human experience is woven with threads of joy, sorrow, defeat, and triumph. Each thread, each experience, is not a random occurrence but a deliberate act of divine intervention. Every moment of joy, every tear shed in sorrow, every defeat, and every victory are all part of a grand design. They are the building blocks that shape us, mold us, and ultimately define who we are. They are the tools used by the divine craftsman to chisel us into the individuals we are meant to be.

God, in His infinite wisdom, mercy, and love, does not merely observe our lives from a distance. He is an active participant, guiding us through the labyrinth of life. He places obstacles in our path that we agreed to but have forgotten, like Job, not to hinder us but to strengthen us. The obstacles are to awaken us to who we truly are. He allows us to experience pain, not to punish us but to teach us resilience. *We live, move, and have our very being in Him.*

He grants us moments of happiness not merely for our enjoyment, but to remind us of the beauty of life's purpose. So that in the end, we would become perfect and completely lacking nothing like our Father.

The divine hand of God is not a puppeteer's hand, controlling our every move. Instead, it is the hand of a loving parent, guiding us, supporting us, and sometimes letting us stumble, so we may learn to pick ourselves up and continue our journey to maturity. The mother eagle does this best with her eaglets.

The experiences we encounter are not random; they are divinely orchestrated. They are the chapters of our life story, written by the most excellent author of all—God. It is like a letter written for the watching world to see, read, and know that we are His workmanship, created and fashioned for His glory and our pre-determined destiny.

This is an inconvenient truth, often overlooked in our quest for understanding. But once we accept it, we begin to see the beauty and divine purpose in every experience, the purpose in every challenge, and the divine love in every moment of our lives.

Before God, the entire creation, visible and invisible, is like a speck. He chose to love us before anything existed. God's love cannot be measured by how much wealth we amass. His passion is evident in the air (His breath) that we breathe. If He holds His breath from the earth, every living thing, including plants, will cease to exist. So far, He hasn't. That is proof of His infinite love toward humanity and His creation. Everything depends on His breath, given to us all from conception. It is the same love that He demonstrated through the sacrifice of His Son for His creation.

His pattern Son instructs us to read about His life in the volume of the book; therein all of Him is written. Yes, in the volume of His book, it is written of Him. *Job's* experience is also written in the volume of his book. *Job's* experience is the experience of every human who has lived, is now living, or will ever live.

It is the experience of every child of the Most High, called according to His purpose, to manifest the fullness of His glory. He desires for us to receive His double portion, which is the portion of God and the portion of man, a double portion to make His sons and daughters complete in Him.

When we are complete in Him, then we have partaken of the fruit of His life, which is His image and nature—knowing good and evil and choosing good. God declared *Job* perfect. He was complete in all dimensions and lacking nothing, by God's estimate. Yes, *Job* was as perfect as he was in the beginning, but he had to be perfected on earth—perfected in spiritual and earthly realms—like El Shaddai, the Father of all perfection.

The critical importance of our *Job experience* has kept God and all those who have gone before us waiting. As they are called, this cloud of witnesses and glory is eagerly waiting, cheering, and rooting for us to finish the race. As the curtain draws to a close, they cannot obtain the promise of perfection until we are made perfect through our *Job* experience.

Even though on the outside looking in, this looked as if it were *Job's* lesson. It was for us all. God will not be denied this promise. His sons and daughters will not be denied the promise. His creation will not be denied the promise either. In the end, *Job* validated God's bragging testimony of him to Satan and confirmed God as being true, and Satan a liar regarding *Job*. Our own '*Job Experience*' will provide further proof. Amen!

In the beginning, the pattern was that the Son was with the Father, in the Father, and was the Father. As the pattern Son was with the Father,

Job was with the Father, and so were we. All human experience was encapsulated in the pattern Son's experience vicariously. The eternal God of love has been our dwelling throughout all generations and before all things. In Him, we live, move, and have our being.

From the beginning, the Almighty created all things by His Son, and all humanity was concealed in Himself, including all principalities and powers in heavenly places, with the intent that God's eternal purpose might be revealed and clearly understood through *Job's* and our experience. Finally, each of us, like all humans, is enveloped in Christ. The Holy Spirit is enveloped in Christ. And Christ is enveloped in God. But God is enveloped in nothing.

The incomprehensible One can be likened to a circle whose center is everywhere and whose circumference has no bounds. *Nothing* exists outside of our Father God. *He envelopes everything and fills it all in all* by Himself! Therefore, after *all things* are made subject to Christ Jesus the Son, as the Father promised him, He, in turn, will present it all to the Father, except Himself who made the promise, He again becomes who He was before the beginning of all things. Glory, Aleluya, Amen!

FINAL WORD

"I am the Alpha and the Omega, the First and the Last, the Beginning and the End."

No suffering or experience will stop the glory of the sons and daughters of Jehovah from being revealed. The promise is sealed with our immutable covenant agreement with the Omnipotent. Job's perfection to double-portion glory is the fulfillment of the promise that the earnest expectation of all creatures had been waiting for through "the manifestation of the sons of God."

Our hope must be rooted in the character of God—His goodness, faithfulness, and love. His Word offers us a beautiful benediction: "May the God of hope fill you with all joy and peace as you trust in him, so that you may overflow with hope by the power of the Holy Spirit." May we continue to trust in God's timing, the assurance of His presence, and the promise of restoration according to His prophetic calendar.

Now, we pray that our Father fulfill His purpose in us and His promise to us as written in our covenants. Father, we thank you for your grace as we continue to grapple with remembering and understanding your purpose in and through the mystery of our individual *human experiences*, such as Job's. In doing so, help us to know, believe, and live in the consciousness of our covenant agreement with You.

May we embrace it as a demonstration of our appreciation for Your love toward us—humanity—that You, in and through Christ, suffered and died for. May the *'It is finished'* declaration by our Savior continue to reveal the mystery of your magnanimous *love*—the love that encompasses all things, framed in eternity, to Your glory.

Praise be unto You, Jehovah God Almighty, that *Job's* experience was but for a season before his restoration and double-portion blessing. Hence, our experience is but for a season before our restoration to our double-portion blessing and glorious destiny in You. It is why we all came to fulfill Your purpose, our purpose.

Our heavenly Father, may You not rest until it is done according to Your original intent. When we see it and know it, may that knowledge and understanding awaken us. Thereby leading each of us to say, *"We are Job indeed."* And in doing so, the mystery of our **"Human Experience"** will no longer be **"An Inconvenient Truth,"** but our reality to embrace and manifest to the fullest as your heart desires!

Thank you, Father!

Questions for Readers

After reading *"Human Experience: An Inconvenient Truth,"*

1. How is the mystery of your human experience shaping you?

2. How will your understanding of the mystery of your human experience help keep you from self-pity, depression, and anger toward others and God and increase your inner peace?

3. How will the revelation of the mystery of your human experience transform you for the better?

4. How will your awareness of the mystery of your human experience reinforce your trust in God, no matter how fierce the experience is?

5. How will the mystery of your human experience, through which you have been restored, strengthened, and established, help others?

6. How will the mystery of your human experience reveal to you an understanding of the purpose of your trials and God's purpose?

7. How will the knowledge of the mystery of your human experience make you aware that God's love is being demonstrated through your experience?

8. Will you continue to ask God Almighty, *'Why me,'* whenever you are experiencing trials and tribulations?

9.   Are you now in a better position to counsel and console the weak who are afflicted and are carrying heavy burdens from the mystery of their human experience?

10. Will you stop blaming family members, friends, and colleagues for being responsible for the extreme inconvenience you are experiencing?

11. Will this knowledge of *"Human Experience: An Inconvenient Truth"* douse your superstitious mindset whenever you are faced with the vicissitudes of life?

12. With the understanding that you have now, are you at a place where you can truly forgive yourself? Also, will you forgive anyone who has hurt you, knowingly or unknowingly? At the same time, they were instrumental in the process of working out your and their covenant toward the glory set before us?

Conclusion

Human experience is a complex, multifaceted enigma that continues to baffle and intrigue us. It is *an inconvenient truth* that we are far from understanding the full depth and breadth of our existence. We are beings of emotion, intellect, and spirit, living in a physical world yet connected to realms beyond our comprehension.

Our experiences, both individual and collective, are shaped by a myriad of factors, from our genetic makeup to our cultural and societal influences. They are shaped by our emotions, thoughts, beliefs, and interactions with others. They are, in essence, the sum of who we are as individuals and as a species.

It serves as a reminder that we are part of a vast, intricate, and beautiful universe, full of mysteries waiting to be explored and unveiled. It is a call to continue seeking, questioning, and embracing the unknown and the unknowable.

Ultimately, our human experience is not a problem to be solved but a journey to be embarked upon and understood by revelation. It is a journey of discovery, growth, and transformation that is as unique and individual as we are, according to our covenant with our Father. And it is this journey, with all its challenges and joys, that truly defines us as human beings with an eternal hope of glory.

Nothing is an accident in our lives. We *knew* it from the beginning and said, *"YES, SEND ME."* And here we are, fulfilling all that we agreed to before we came into this world. Hopefully, *"Human Experience"* should no longer be a mystery but will remain *"An Inconvenient Truth"* that we embrace triumphantly with courage, according to our purpose written in our covenant agreement, or the volume of our book, with our heavenly Father being fulfilled.

Amen!

A Recap of Human Experience: An Inconvenient Truth

This work, *Human Experience: An Inconvenient Truth,* by God's grace, explores the profound spiritual and existential journey of human experience through the lens of the biblical figure Job. It presents life as a divine covenant and a purposeful journey marked by trials, suffering, faith, and eventual restoration, emphasizing the intricate relationship between divine sovereignty and human endurance.

Introduction to Human Experience as an Inconvenient Truth and Job's Story

This book frames human experience as a complex mystery intertwined with divine purpose, where suffering, pain, and joy are part of a grander design in awe and reverential fear of God's Omnipotence. It uses Job's life as a universal metaphor for all people, highlighting how trials serve to reveal deeper spiritual truths and prepare individuals for their ultimate purpose and restoration. The narrative stresses that life's hardships are not random but are part of a covenant with God, orchestrated with divine timing and precision.

The Appointed Time of Obscurity

The initial chapters discuss a period of obscurity and suffering, termed the "*Job experience*," where individuals feel undervalued, isolated, and face intense trials. This phase is likened to a seed buried in darkness before growth, emphasizing that such obscurity is necessary for spiritual development and fulfillment of divine purposes. The text describes a heavenly council where God appoints assignments, including trials permitted to Satan, illustrating the divine orchestration behind earthly experiences. God uses our time of obscurity, not as a delay, but to orchestrate and prepare us to be ready and aligned with our ordained purpose according to our covenant agreement with Him.

The Assignment and the Test

A detailed account of the divine conversation between God and Satan sets the stage for Job's trials. Satan challenges Job's faithfulness, suggesting it is contingent on his prosperity and protection. God allows Satan to take Job's possessions and family, but prohibits him from harming Job directly. The narrative portrays Job's steadfast worship and faith despite devastating losses, underscoring the theme of trust amid suffering. Similar spiritual battles and divine covenants are noted as ongoing realities for all humanity. God loves you too much to leave you unchallenged; ask Abraham, Jacob, Moses, Joseph, Hannah, Jeremiah, Esther, David, Paul, and the list goes on. He chastises whom He loves, and who is destined for a beyond-ordinary purpose.

Timing and Location in Divine Purpose

This book emphasizes that all events in life occur according to divine timing and place, reinforcing that nothing happens by accident. The meaning of Job's name and the land of Uz are explored, symbolizing endurance, restoration, and divine counsel, further illustrating how

God's choices in timing and location serve His greater plan. Examples from biblical and historical figures reinforce the concept of divinely appointed seasons and places for fulfilling God's purpose.

Purpose Behind Trials

The narrative returns to the heavenly council, where God permits Satan to afflict Job's body, intensifying his trials to test his faith further. Job's experience reveals hidden fears and attachments, ultimately leading to repentance and freedom to worship God authentically. The text highlights that trials serve to refine character, reveal true faith, and fulfill divine covenant, transcending mere punishment or random suffering.

Faithfulness and Trust Amidst Suffering

Job's friends arrive to console him, but soon question his righteousness, reflecting common human responses to suffering. This book discusses how faithfulness does not exempt one from trials but is tested and deepened through them. It encourages readers to trust God's sovereignty and view trials as opportunities for growth and deeper intimacy with God rather than as punishments. Enduring hardship through long suffering builds character and strengthens faith.

Divine Wisdom and Human Understanding

A significant portion focuses on the search for divine wisdom, which surpasses human understanding. God's response to Job, highlighting the vastness of creation and human limitations, teaches humility and trust in divine sovereignty. The youngest friend, Elihu, rebukes the others for their inadequate counsel, emphasizing that true wisdom comes from God alone. The text invites readers to seek wisdom through prayer and scripture, aligning with God's purposes.

God's Omnipotence and Sovereignty

The omnipotence of God is portrayed as foundational, with creation and human affairs under His control. God's power sustains life and orchestrates history, including permitting trials within set boundaries. Job's restoration exemplifies God's redemptive power. This book's narrative stresses reliance on God's strength and trust in His sovereign will, even when circumstances are incomprehensible.

Patience and Restoration

Job's story culminates in a turning point marked by repentance, humility, and intercession for his friends. God's patience allows human wisdom to reach its limits before revealing divine truth. Job's comprehensive restoration—including doubled wealth, new children, and longevity—illustrates God's faithfulness and the reward of steadfast faith. The text encourages patience and trust in God's timing, recognizing suffering as a process toward ultimate blessing.

Knowledge, Endurance, and Victory

Endurance is presented as essential for spiritual maturity. Job's perseverance amid trials exemplifies hopeful trust in God's justice. The example of Jesus Christ underscores endurance through submission to

God's will, as outlined in His covenant with His Father before the foundation of the world. The text advocates strengthening faith through prayer, scripture, fellowship, and worship, emphasizing active faith expressed in daily life. Our capacity to remain steadfast through adversity is manifested by the endurance gained from knowledge, which leads us to victory.

Ever-Present God and Eternal Perspective

This book's narrative highlights the limitation of focusing solely on temporal experiences and encourages adopting an eternal perspective. Assurance of God's constant presence provides comfort during suffering. Job's faith shifts toward hope in ultimate redemption and seeing God face-to-face. Living with an eternal outlook fosters gratitude, contentment, and purposeful engagement in God's kingdom work.

Infinite Love and Ultimate Purpose

God's love is described as infinite and active in refining believers through trials, conforming them to Christ's image. Job's experience symbolizes this transformative journey, drawing individuals into deeper intimacy with God. The divine purpose encompasses molding character, preparing for eternal life, and manifesting God's glory. Human experiences, including long suffering and joy, are integral to this divine craftsmanship. But suffering long is not God's desire for anyone, because it is self-imposed.

Final Reflections and Application

The concluding sections affirm that suffering and trials are part of the divine covenant and necessary for the revelation of God's glory in believers. The narrative calls readers to embrace their *"Job experience"* courageously, trusting in God's promises and timing. It offers reflective questions to encourage personal application and spiritual growth, emphasizing forgiveness, trust, and the recognition of God's sovereign plan in all human experience.

God's Ultimate Purpose

This comprehensive spiritual reflection uses Job's story as a framework to understand human suffering, divine purpose, and the journey toward restoration and glory. It underscores the importance of faithfulness, long-suffering, endurance, patience, wisdom, and eternal perspective in navigating life's challenges according to a divine covenant established before birth and accomplishing God's ultimate purpose.

God loves you too much to leave you unchallenged; ask Abraham, Jacob, Moses, Joseph, Hannah, Jeremiah, Esther, David, Paul, and the list goes on. He chastises whom He loves, and who is destined for a beyond-ordinary purpose. Therefore, this work invites readers to view their experiences as part of a greater divine narrative, fostering hope, trust, and transformation, all to the glory of God, who fills all in all. Amen!

PRAYER OF SUBMISSION AND TRUST

Forever, O Lord, Your Word is firmly established in the heavens.

May Your Word continue to be a lamp to my feet and a light to my path daily.

Lord, remember Your Word to me, Your servant, in which You have made me hope and trust daily.

O Lord, teach me daily that I may know Your status and the power of Your love and grace.

Give me understanding and lead me in the way of Your commandments and Your will daily.

Open my eyes of understanding so that I may continually behold the wondrous things out of Your law and Your eternal vision and purpose encapsulated in Christ Jesus, my Lord.

Lord, guide me, guard me, lead me, and direct me daily by the light of the Holy Spirit.

May Your hand be with me to keep me close to You and hide me in Your pavilion.

Thank you, Father, in the matchless name of my Lord and Savior, Jesus Christ.

Amen!